Generis
PUBLISHING

Integration of Artificial Intelligence in Criminal Investigation and Criminal Proceedings

Tatia Dolidze

Title: **Integration of Artificial Intelligence in Criminal Investigation and Criminal Proceedings**

ISBN: 979-8-89966-347-5

Author: Tatia Dolidze

Cover image: www.pixabay.com

Publisher: Generis Publishing
Online orders: www.generis-publishing.com
Contact email: info@generis-publishing.com

Integration of Artificial Intelligence in Criminal Investigation and Criminal Proceedings

Tatia Dolidze, Doctor of Law

Contents

Preface

> "Technology is neither good nor bad; its value depends on its use."
> — *Melvin Kranzberg*

The rapid advancement of artificial intelligence (AI) over the past decade has become one of the most significant technological phenomena of modern civilization. Its impact extends far beyond mere technical innovation, directly influencing legal systems, the organization of social relations, and models of state governance. This transformation is particularly visible in the field of criminal law, where AI is already being applied to optimize investigations, analyze and evaluate evidence, support law enforcement operations, and accelerate judicial decision-making.

The integration of AI into criminal law raises not only technological but also legal and ethical questions: How can the innovation potential be aligned with the protection of fundamental human rights? How can we ensure objectivity and avoid algorithmic bias? How can we achieve transparency and maintain public trust without hindering innovation? This work is intended not only for legal professionals but also for all those interested in the legal, technological, and ethical aspects of AI — including information technology specialists, data protection experts, policymakers, researchers, and students. It offers historical, theoretical, and practical analysis, providing readers with a comprehensive understanding of AI's use in criminal law.

In the realm of criminal justice, crime prevention is of utmost importance. Experience shows that this goal cannot be achieved solely through stricter legislation — it requires faster, more efficient legal processes and a robust evidentiary base in today's reality, where investigations and trials often last months or even years, AI presents an unprecedented opportunity to accelerate and simplify these procedures.

The purpose of this study is not only to review existing international and national regulations but also to demonstrate that artificial intelligence is not a temporary technological trend. Rather, it is a powerful tool which, when governed by appropriate legal and ethical frameworks, can become a vital ally of law enforcement systems — serving public safety and crime prevention.

Special attention is devoted to data protection, human oversight, and algorithmic transparency, as these elements form the cornerstone of public trust. The work also provides recommendations to improve policy, legislation, and practice to ensure that AI implementation in the legal sphere remains fair and human rights-oriented.

Ultimately, this study serves as a call for a broader dialogue — one that unites lawyers, engineers, policymakers, and citizens alike. Artificial intelligence is already part of our legal reality. Now, its use must promote not only efficiency but also justice and the safety of society.

Introduction

Over the past decades, digital technologies have radically transformed the field of law. This transformation is evident across all branches of legal science, yet its impact is particularly notable in criminal investigation and criminal justice. It would not be an exaggeration to say that artificial intelligence (AI) has emerged as a powerful new instrument for investigative and judicial systems.

Modern states increasingly rely on algorithmic systems not only for crime prevention but also for identifying offenders and evaluating evidence. Against this backdrop, questions about the legality of AI integration into the justice system and its compatibility with fundamental human rights principles have become more pressing than ever.

Today, artificial intelligence is actively used by law enforcement agencies, particularly in the following areas:

- Through predictive policing models, which aim to identify potential crimes based on statistical data;[1]
- By means of facial recognition technologies, used for the identification and surveillance of suspects;[2]
- Through automated risk assessment algorithms used in courts, which often determine the likelihood of pretrial detention or probation release.[3]

Opportunities, concerns are growing regarding algorithmic bias, the preservation of evidentiary standards, and the risk of human rights violations.[4] This is precisely why it is essential to strengthen legal frameworks and implement transparent mechanisms

---

[1] Brantingham, J. P., Valasik, M., & Mohler, G. O. (2018). Does predictive policing lead to biased arrests? *Statistics and Public Policy*, 5(1), 1–6. https://doi.org/10.1080/2330443X.2018.1438940 (last accessed 1.08.2025).

[2] Garvie, C., Bedoya, A., & Frankle, J. (2016). *The perpetual lineup: Unregulated police face recognition in America.* Georgetown Law Center on Privacy & Technology. https://www.perpetuallineup.org/ (last accessed 1.08.2025)

[3] Wachter, S., Mittelstadt, B., & Floridi, L. (2017). Transparent, explainable, and accountable AI for robotics. *Science Robotics*, 2(6), eaan6080. https://doi.org/10.1126/scirobotics.aan6080 (last accessed 1.08.2025)

[4] Ibid.

to ensure that the integration of artificial intelligence into criminal proceedings does not contradict the fundamental principles of justice.

The purpose of this study is to analyze the possible forms and aspects through which artificial intelligence is applied in criminal proceedings, from the investigation stage to judicial review. The research focuses both on the technological capabilities of AI and the legal and ethical challenges associated with its use. The study covers the historical development of artificial intelligence, its initial introduction into law, international experience, and the current situation.

The research methodology is based on a mixed-methods approach, employing dogmatic-normative analysis (document and legislative review), the comparative legal method, and inductive-deductive reasoning to evaluate specific technological models and practices.

This work represents an attempt to assess the compatibility between technology and the legal system—to determine whether it is possible to achieve greater efficiency in investigation and adjudication without compromising individual rights and interests.

Chapter I. The History, Concept, and Classification of Artificial Intelligence

1.1. The Birth of the Thinking Machine

The classical definition of artificial intelligence encompasses systems capable of performing tasks that normally require human intelligence. One of the pioneers in this field, John McCarthy, who is credited with coining the term *"artificial intelligence,"* defined it as follows: "Artificial Intelligence is the science and engineering of making intelligent machines." This formulation captures the dual essence of AI — as both a scientific discipline aimed at understanding intelligence itself and an engineering endeavor focused on replicating intelligent behavior through machines.[5]

Artificial intelligence can be classified into several types:

- Narrow AI – specialized systems designed to perform a single specific task (for example, facial recognition).
- Strong AI / General AI – hypothetical systems capable of fully replicating human intelligence across all domains.
- Superintelligence – a theoretical concept referring to levels of AI capability that surpass human intelligence by far.[6]

In today's reality, only Narrow AI is used in practice — including within law enforcement and judicial systems.

Today, artificial intelligence (AI) is regarded as the hallmark of the modern digital era. However, the idea itself is far older than computer technology. As early as antiquity, the notion of mechanical, human-like beings endowed with abilities resembling those of humans and capable of acting in a similar manner existed. For instance, in Greek mythology, there was the legendary Talos — a giant bronze figure often described as an *"iron colossus,"* Talos was said to have been created by Hephaestus, the god of craftsmanship, and was programmed with specific instructions: to circle the island of Crete three times a day and protect it from potential invaders.[7]

---

[5] McCarthy, J. (2007). What is artificial intelligence? [Online manuscript]. http://jmc.stanford.edu/articles/whatisai/whatisai.pdf (last accessed: 1.08.2025)

[6] Bostrom, N. (2014). *Superintelligence: Paths, dangers, strategies.* Oxford University Press.

[7] Apollonius Rhodius. (2007). *Argonautica* (R. Hunter, Trans.). Oxford University Press. (Original work published ca. 3rd century BCE).

According to the myth, Talos had a single vein running through his entire body, filled with *ichor* (ἰχώρ) — the divine fluid that gave him life. This vein was sealed with a metal nail, and removing it would deactivate the giant. His actions were entirely controlled by human-given instructions, resembling a primitive form of coding or programming. This functional characteristic makes Talos the first mythological robot and a precursor to the modern concept of artificial intelligence. In the classical source of the myth, Apollonius of Rhodes' *Argonautica*, it is described how Medea defeated Talos by using deception—she tricked him into removing the nail, causing the divine fluid to drain from his body and rendering the giant lifeless.[8] A phenomenon that today could be equated to a system malfunction resulting in functional failure.[9]

For this reason, both early authors and modern scholars regard Talos as a prototype of the first technological creation. The American historian Adrienne Mayor, in her work *"Gods and Robots,"* presents Talos not merely as a mechanical being but as a "programmed guardian" operating according to a predefined code.[10] This analysis indicates that the concept of creating a human-like device is not a recent phenomenon; instead, its roots can be traced back to the ancient Greek Hellenistic period.

1.2. The First Breath of the Algorithm

The modern history of artificial intelligence begins in the mid-20th century. The early work of pioneering scientists was primarily based on logic and mathematical models. The idea that a machine could think was first proposed by the mathematician Alan Turing (1912–1954).

In 1950, Turing published his groundbreaking paper *"Computing Machinery and Intelligence,"* in which he introduced the concept of the Turing Test — a method for determining whether a machine can exhibit human-like intelligence. According to this test, if a machine can engage in a conversation with a human being in such a way that the person cannot tell whether they are communicating with another human or with a

---

[8] Apollonius Rhodius. (2007). *Argonautica* (R. Hunter, Trans.). Oxford University Press. (Original work published ca. 3rd century BCE).

[9] Murray, A. T. (Trans.). (1919). *Apollonius Rhodius: Argonautica*. Loeb Classical Library. Harvard University Press.

[10] Mayor, A. (2018). *Gods and Robots: Myths, Machines, and Ancient Dreams of Technology*. Princeton University Press.

machine, then it may be said that the machine "thinks" — that is, demonstrates intelligence.[11]

The formal birthdate of artificial intelligence as an independent discipline is considered to be 1956, when the renowned Dartmouth Summer Research Project on Artificial Intelligence took place. During this conference, John McCarthy, who chaired the event, posed a fundamental question to the scientific community: "Let us study how to make machines use language, form abstractions and concepts, solve kinds of problems now reserved for humans, and improve themselves." At this conference, McCarthy first introduced the term "artificial intelligence," which would later define an entire scientific field — one for which he is now recognized as the founding father of AI.[12]

The same conference brought together some of the most prominent scientists of the time, including Marvin Minsky, Allen Newell, Herbert Simon, and Claude Shannon. This historic gathering laid the foundation for a new and innovative scientific field — one that would continue to evolve and shape research for decades to come.[13]

From the 1960s to the 1970s, the development of artificial intelligence largely progressed along rule-based lines. During this period, systems were created to solve problems within specific domains — such as mathematics, medicine, and law — using predefined sets of rules created by humans.

One of the first such programs was the Logic Theorist (1956), which aimed to automatically generate proofs of formal logic theorems. This marked a significant milestone in demonstrating that logical reasoning, previously considered an exclusively human capacity, could be simulated by a machine.[14]

---

[11] A. M. Turing (1950) Computing Machinery and Intelligence. Mind 49: 433-460, https://courses.cs.umbc.edu/471/papers/turing.pdf (last accessed: 5.08.2025)

[12] McCarthy, J., Minsky, M. L., Rochester, N., & Shannon, C. E. (1955). *A proposal for the Dartmouth summer research project on artificial intelligence.* http://jmc.stanford.edu/articles/dartmouth/dartmouth.pdf (last accessed: 5.08.2025)

[13] J. McCarthy, Dartmouth College M. L. Minsky, Harvard University N. Rochester, I.B.M. Corporation C.E. Shannon, Bell Telephone Laboratorie, Darthmouth Summer Research Project on Artificial Intelligence http://jmc.stanford.edu/articles/dartmouth/dartmouth.pdf (last accessed: 5.08.2025).

[14] Newell, A., & Simon, H. A. (1956). The logic theory machine—a complex information processing system. *IRE Transactions on Information Theory*, 2(3), 61–79. https://doi.org/10.1109/TIT.1956.1056810 (last accessed 5.08.2025).

It was followed by the General Problem Solver (GPS) — a more general system concept designed to construct logical structures to achieve a given goal. This program represented an essential step toward creating machines capable of applying reasoning strategies to a broad range of problems, rather than being confined to a single specialized task.[15]

In the 1960s, specialized systems began to emerge for specific fields. For example, DENDRAL (1965), developed in the field of chemistry, performed structural analysis of compounds based on expert knowledge, while ELIZA (1966) represented a symbolically modeled psychotherapeutic chatbot capable of communicating with users in natural language. These systems demonstrated, for the first time, that artificial intelligence could emulate not only logical reasoning but also aspects of human communication and domain-specific expertise.[16]

In the field of law, one of the first true expert systems was TAXMAN (1977), developed within the context of U.S. tax law. This system was designed to model legal reasoning, mimicking a lawyer's logical decision-making process on specific issues by analyzing existing rules and precedents. The system operated on the following principles:

- It employed a rule-based reasoning model;
- Legal precedents were represented as formal logical structures;
- The system analyzed the facts of a case, compared them with existing precedents, and determined which legal principles should be applied.
- One of its key innovations was the simulation of analogical reasoning (case-based reasoning), allowing the system to conclude by comparing new cases with previously decided ones.[17]

This system was practically a pioneer in the field of law, demonstrating that a so-called *thinking machine* could not only retrieve information but also structurally model legal argumentation. Later, beginning in the 1980s, more advanced systems emerged — such as HYPO, which applied analogical reasoning based on case law and enabled

[15] Newell, A., Shaw, J. C., & Simon, H. A. (1959). Report on a general problem-solving program. In *Proceedings of the International Conference on Information Processing* (pp. 256–264). UNESCO.
[16] Buchanan, B. G., & Feigenbaum, E. A. (1978). DENDRAL and Meta-DENDRAL: Their applications dimension. *Artificial Intelligence*, 11(1–2), 5–24. https://doi.org/10.1016/0004-3702(78)90007-0 (last accessed: 5.08.2025).
[17] McCarty, L. T. (1977). Reflections on "taxman": An experiment in artificial intelligence and legal reasoning. *Harvard Law Review*, 90(5), 837–893.

modeling hypothetical legal arguments. These developments marked a significant step toward the creation of AI systems capable of supporting complex legal analysis and reasoning processes.[18]

These programs represented the initial stages of artificial intelligence's evolution, laying the groundwork for the modern integration of AI into the field of law — including the development of automated models for investigation, forensic examination, and judicial analysis. However, it should also be noted that due to the limited computational capacity of computers at the time and the lack of sufficient data, the large-scale implementation of these systems faced significant challenges and constraints.

1.3. Stagnation and the "Winter" of Artificial Intelligence

The 1970s marked a turning point in the development of artificial intelligence. After an initial wave of optimism and enthusiasm, both the scientific community and society at large faced a period of technological disillusionment. Although the 1956 Dartmouth Conference and subsequent logical models had created the impression that the creation of fully functioning "cognitive machines" was imminent, reality told a different story.

What had been envisioned as a rapid, transformative technological revolution instead became a phase marked by high expectations but little tangible progress — a period that came to be known as the "first AI winter,".[19]

Several essential factors caused the slowdown in the development of AI systems:

[18] Ashley, K. D. (1990). *Modeling legal argument: Reasoning with cases and hypotheticals*. MIT Press.

[19] Crevier, D. (1993). *AI: The Tumultuous History of the Search for Artificial Intelligence*. Basic Books.

1. Technological limitations: The expert systems developed in the 1960s, such as Logic Theorist[20], General Problem Solver[21], and later DENDRAL[22] — were based on rule-based models. However, these systems required an enormous amount of manually entered information (rule-based knowledge), which significantly limited their scalability and made their practical implementation highly labor-intensive.
2. Reduction of financial resources: The initial funding provided by the U.S. Department of Defense and DARPA (Defense Advanced Research Projects Agency) was tied to the expectation of practical and timely results. When AI systems failed to deliver effective outcomes—particularly in natural language processing and general intelligence—funding was drastically reduced. This shift became especially evident after 1969, when DARPA adopted a more skeptical stance toward basic, theory-driven research, prioritizing projects with immediate military or practical applications instead.[23]
3. Shift in priorities and public backlash: In 1973, the British government published the well-known Lighthill Report, which offered a highly critical assessment of AI's progress, stating that the field had failed to meet scientific expectations, particularly in areas involving human-like cognitive performance. The report concluded that AI research was producing limited practical results compared to the resources invested. As a result, funding for AI research in the United Kingdom was significantly reduced, which in turn influenced broader European attitudes, leading to a general decline in institutional and financial support for artificial intelligence across the region.[24]
4. The problem of knowledge transfer to machines: Another major challenge concerned the question of how to transfer human knowledge about the world to machines in a way that would allow them to interpret it correctly. In many cases, systems would fail or stop functioning altogether when faced with even minor structural changes in input data, unable to generate decisions in open or dynamic

---

[20] Newell, A., & Simon, H. A. (1956). The logic theory machine—a complex information processing system. *IRE Transactions on Information Theory*, 2(3), 61–79. https://doi.org/10.1109/TIT.1956.1056810 (last accessed: 10.08.2025).

[21] Newell, A., Shaw, J. C., & Simon, H. A. (1959). Report on a general problem-solving program. In *Proceedings of the International Conference on Information Processing* (pp. 256–264). UNESCO.

[22] Buchanan, B. G., & Feigenbaum, E. A. (1978). DENDRAL and Meta-DENDRAL: Their applications dimension. *Artificial Intelligence*, 11(1–2), 5–24. https://doi.org/10.1016/0004-3702(78)90007-0 (last accessed: 10.08.2025).

[23] Nilsson, N. J. (1998). *Artificial Intelligence: A New Synthesis*. Morgan Kaufmann.

[24] Lighthill, J. (1973). *Artificial Intelligence: A General Survey*. In *Artificial Intelligence: A paper symposium* (pp. 1–20). Science Research Council, UK.

environments. The so-called "AI winter" was not, in fact, a complete technological regression but rather a temporary collapse in the realization of overly optimistic forecasts — caused by both technical limitations and managerial overconfidence. However, this period provided a crucial learning experience for future development: it accelerated the exploration of alternative approaches, particularly machine learning, which later, in the 1990s, laid the foundation for the modern resurgence of artificial intelligence. [25] Therefore, the first AI winter can be described as an era of unrealized ideas—a time when technological potential existed. Still, the necessary technical and institutional foundations for sustainable progress had not yet been established.

1.4. The Renaissance of Neurons: A New Life in Artificial Intelligence

After the first AI winter, scientists and the technological sector approached the development and application of artificial intelligence with considerable caution. The failures of earlier decades were largely attributed to overinflated expectations and weak technological infrastructure.

However, by the late 2000s and especially during the 2010s, the field of artificial intelligence underwent a remarkable and systemic transformation, laying the foundation for what has often been called the "second life" of AI. This new era is symbolically referred to as the "awakening of neurons," directly linked to the technological revolution of deep neural networks.

Deep neural networks are multi-layered algorithmic structures inspired by the functioning of the human brain, designed to recognize complex patterns in data and to uncover connections that traditional algorithms often overlook.[26] These models enabled groundbreaking achievements, including:

- Automatic image recognition (computer vision);
- Speech and text processing (natural language processing);
- Machine translation;
- Recommendation systems;

---

[25] Russell, S. J., & Norvig, P. (2021). *Artificial Intelligence: A Modern Approach* (4th ed.). Pearson.
[26] LeCun, Y., Bengio, Y., & Hinton, G. (2015). Deep learning. *Nature*, 521(7553), 436–444. https://doi.org/10.1038/nature14539 (last accessed: 10.08.2025).

- Performance in games at or above human level.

Several key factors proved decisive in enabling these breakthroughs:

- Automatic image recognition (computer vision);
- Speech and text processing (natural language processing);
- Machine translation;
- Recommendation systems;
- Human-level or superior performance in games.

Several key factors proved decisive in this process:

1. Availability of large-scale data (Big Data) – provides the vast amounts of material necessary for training artificial intelligence systems;
2. Increase in computational power (GPUs, cloud computing) – made it possible to run and optimize deep learning models efficiently;
3. Advancement of mathematical algorithms – including techniques such as gradient descent, backpropagation, and others that refined model training and performance.

One of the most renowned events that brought this technology to worldwide recognition occurred during the 2012 ImageNet competition, where a deep neural network model, AlexNet, developed by Alex Krizhevsky, Ilya Sutskever, and Geoffrey Hinton, achieved significantly superior results compared to all previous models. This breakthrough demonstrated the transformative potential of deep learning, marking a decisive moment in the modern history of artificial intelligence and paving the way for its widespread adoption across multiple scientific and practical domains.[27]

The success of deep neural networks facilitated the return of artificial intelligence not merely as an experimental concept, but as a practical tool integrated across various domains — including law enforcement, medicine, finance, and legal systems. This phenomenon is often compared to a Renaissance ("AI Renaissance") in art and science — a period when ideas once stalled were revived in a new technological context. It was precisely the "awakening" of deep neural networks that transformed artificial

[27] Krizhevsky, A., Sutskever, I., & Hinton, G. E. (2012). ImageNet classification with deep convolutional neural networks. *Communications of the ACM*, 60(6), 84–90. https://doi.org/10.1145/3065386 (last accessed: 15.08.2025).

intelligence from a vision of the future into a tool of the present, redefining the relationship between human cognition and machine capability.[28]

1.5. The Crossroads of Law and Artificial Intelligence: The Initial Stage

Although the early focus of artificial intelligence research was primarily on technical disciplines, the field of law soon attracted the attention of AI researchers. Early experiments sought to model legal reasoning, algorithmize decision-making, and simulate argumentation based on precedent analysis. These pioneering systems laid the foundation for modern legal technologies, which are now applied in both investigative and judicial processes.

As mentioned earlier, one of the first and most significant experiments in this domain was TAXMAN (1977), developed by Layman McCarty at Harvard University. The system aimed to interpret corporate tax law norms within the U.S. tax regulatory framework. It was capable of performing legal categorization and determining the legal class of individual cases according to predefined rules, thereby marking one of the earliest successful attempts to formalize legal reasoning through artificial intelligence. [29]

A second major milestone was HYPO (developed in the late 1980s by Kevin Ashley at the University of Pittsburgh). HYPO was based on case-based reasoning (CBR), a method of legal argumentation grounded in analogies between judicial decisions. The system generated hypothetical cases, compared them with past precedents, and provided users with argumentation templates for legal reasoning.[30] HYPO thus laid the foundation for the intelligent modeling of judicial argumentation, representing a crucial step toward the development of modern AI-assisted legal analysis tools.

This approach was further expanded by CATO (1992–1995), also developed by Kevin Ashley in collaboration with Vincent Aleven. Designed primarily for law students, CATO assisted users in comparing arguments between precedent cases,

---

[28] Russell, S. J., & Norvig, P. (2021). *Artificial Intelligence: A Modern Approach* (4th ed.). Pearson.

[29] McCarty, L. T. (1977). Reflections on "TAXMAN": An experiment in artificial intelligence and legal reasoning. *Harvard Law Review*, 90(5), 837–893. https://doi.org/10.2307/1340317 (last accessed: 15.08.2025).

[30] Ashley, K. D. (1990). *Modelling legal argument: Reasoning with cases and hypotheticals*. MIT Press.

conducting hypothetical analyses, and constructing legal positions.[31] It became one of the first AI systems to be practically applied in legal education, serving as an interactive learning tool that demonstrated how artificial intelligence could support the development of analytical reasoning and argumentation skills in legal study.

Later, toward the end of the 2000s, a significant step toward standardizing legal knowledge was taken through the European Union's ESTRELLA Project (2006–2010). The project aimed to develop a framework for the exchange of legal knowledge and to advance tools for the digital processing of legislative texts. Within the scope of ESTRELLA, the Legal Knowledge Interchange Format (LKIF) was created — a standardized format that ensures compatibility between different legal models and provides a foundation for the development of advanced legal expert systems. This initiative represented a significant move toward the interoperability and digital integration of legal information across jurisdictions.[32]

In parallel, the United States introduced the COMPAS system (*Correctional Offender Management Profiling for Alternative Sanctions*), an automated risk assessment tool designed to predict the likelihood of recidivism among defendants. It was used in the judicial process as an auxiliary instrument to assist in decision-making regarding sentencing and parole. However, in 2016, ProPublica published a critical analysis revealing potential bias within the system, particularly concerning racial and socioeconomic factors.[33] This case became a notable example of the need for integrating artificial intelligence into law, requiring not only technological precision but also ethical and legal vigilance to ensure fairness, transparency, and respect for fundamental rights.

One of the most recent and groundbreaking experiments is the so-called "robot judge," which has been operating in Estonia in a testing phase since 2019. The system is designed to review and decide low-value civil disputes under human supervision automatically. This represents the first state-supported initiative to automate judicial

---

[31] Aleven, V., & Ashley, K. D. (1997). Teaching case-based argumentation through interactive multimedia. *Artificial Intelligence and Law*, 5(2–4), 193–218. https://doi.org/10.1023/A:1008292512206 (last accessed: 20.08.2025).

[32] Breuker, J., et al. (2009). The ESTRELLA project: Standardizing legal knowledge. *Knowledge Engineering Review*, 24(3), 251–275. https://doi.org/10.1017/S0269888909990096 (last accessed: 20.08.2025).

[33] Angwin, J., Larson, J., Mattu, S., & Kirchner, L. (2016). Machine bias. *ProPublica*. https://www.propublica.org/article/machine-bias-risk-assessments-in-criminal-sentencing (last accessed: 20.08.2025).

functions, marking a historic step toward the potential use of artificial intelligence in formal decision-making within the judiciary.[34]

The early experiments with artificial intelligence in law can be characterized as technological laboratory attempts that, despite their technical limitations, were transformative for modeling legal reasoning. These systems acted as a bridge between law and algorithmic data processing, creating a foundation that reshaped both legal education and the strategic planning of legal practice.

It thus becomes clear that the concept of artificial intelligence is not a purely modern invention — its roots lie in ancient mythology. As seen in the example of Talos, early humans imagined an artificially created "protector" that operated according to predetermined rules — effectively a prototype of a programmed machine.

In the 20th century, as scientists such as Alan Turing and participants in the Dartmouth Conference began to give this idea an algorithmic form, AI evolved from a technological curiosity into an independent scientific discipline. From the outset, it was evident that artificial intelligence posed not only technological challenges but also a complex of scientific, theoretical, and philosophical problems.

The developmental cycle of AI reveals a repeating pattern — initial enthusiasm, high expectations, disillusionment, and eventual renewal. The so-called "first AI winter" serves as a reminder of how excessive optimism and unrealistic expectations can halt progress. Yet, that very stagnation inspired the emergence of new paradigms such as machine learning and deep neural networks, ushering in AI's "second life."

From a legal perspective, it is particularly significant that law was among the first domains targeted by AI research. Systems such as TAXMAN, HYPO, CATO, and later ESTRELLA, COMPAS, and the "robot judge" in Estonia all demonstrate the law's intrinsic demand for structured reasoning and formal logic, which naturally aligns with the principles governing AI. However, these same systems also highlighted the risks of AI integration into legal frameworks — including bias, lack of transparency, and the need for ethical and procedural safeguards.

Consequently, the evolution of artificial intelligence has been neither linear nor unbroken — it has advanced through cycles of innovation and crisis, progress and regression. What this history teaches us is that technological progress alone cannot

[34] Surden, H. (2020). Artificial Intelligence and Law: An Overview. In *Cambridge Handbook of the Law of Algorithms* (pp. 277–301). Cambridge University Press.

produce true transformation. Philosophical insight, ethical foundations, and clear legal frameworks must accompany it.

Ultimately, the integration of AI into law is not merely a technical or innovative issue — it represents a profound challenge of values: the task of harmonizing efficiency, justice, and human rights within a coherent legal order.

Chapter II. Integration of Artificial Intelligence into Criminal Investigation

2.1. Facial and Object Recognition Systems

One of the most widely used and controversial applications of Artificial Intelligence (AI) today is facial and object recognition technology. These systems are utilized in both the public and private sectors, including law enforcement and judicial institutions. Their foundation lies in modern deep neural networks (DNNs), particularly convolutional neural networks (CNNs), which enable the processing and interpretation of visual information.

Facial recognition systems automate the biometric identification of individuals. AI algorithms are trained on thousands or even millions of facial features — such as the distance between the eyes, the angle of the jaw, and facial symmetry — to generate a unique biometric profile. Some of the most well-known systems include:

- FaceNet (Google)
- DeepFace (Meta/Facebook)
- Face++ (Megvii, China)

Object detection systems such as YOLO, SSD, and Faster R-CNN can rapidly detect and classify specific objects (e.g., weapons, vehicles, human bodies) in photos or video frames. These technologies are integrated into modern surveillance cameras, drones, and smart city infrastructures.

AI-based facial and object recognition technologies are used in law enforcement for:

- Border control (e.g., the U.S. Department of Homeland Security uses facial recognition systems in airports);
- Identification of detainees (recognition of individuals in video footage);
- Search and identification of wanted suspects — automated facial comparison with police databases.

For instance, in London, the Metropolitan Police has been using Live Facial Recognition (LFR) systems in public spaces since 2020. During one such operation, the faces of more than 70,000 individuals were digitally scanned — an event that sparked intense criticism from British media and human rights organizations (BBC, 2020).

In China, the Skynet system is considered the world's largest facial recognition network. As of 2022, more than 700 million surveillance cameras operate across the country, monitoring cities in real time. This vast infrastructure enables law enforcement agencies to rapidly identify and track suspects, providing an unprecedented level of control and surveillance within public spaces.[35]

In the United States, the FBI's facial recognition system, known as NGI-IPS (*Next Generation Identification – Interstate Photo System*), maintains an archive containing millions of facial images used to assist in criminal investigations. However, in 2019, the American Civil Liberties Union (ACLU) published a report stating that the system exhibited a significantly higher error rate when identifying Black and Asian individuals compared to white individuals, raising serious concerns about algorithmic bias and discrimination within law enforcement technologies.[36]

Despite their potential, facial and object recognition systems raise numerous legal, ethical, and human rights concerns, including:

1. **Biased outcomes** – Studies have shown that systems such as *Amazon Rekognition* produce significantly higher error rates when identifying **women**, **Black individuals**, and other **minority groups**.[37]
2. **Excessive surveillance** – Cameras often monitor not only suspects but also **innocent citizens**, infringing on **constitutional rights**, including the freedoms of **privacy, assembly, and expression**.
3. **Divergent regulations and standards** – In some EU Member States, such as **France** and **Germany**, the use of facial recognition in public spaces is **severely restricted or entirely banned**.

[35] Feldstein, S. (2019). The Global Expansion of AI Surveillance. *Carnegie Endowment for International Peace.* https://carnegieendowment.org/2019/09/17/global-expansion-of-ai-surveillance-pub-79847 (Last access: 10.08.2025 წ.).

[36] Garvie, C., Bedoya, A. M., & Frankle, J. (2016). *The Perpetual Line-Up: Unregulated Police Face Recognition in America.* Georgetown Law Center on Privacy & Technology. https://www.perpetuallineup.org (Last access: 10.08.2025 წ.).

[37] Buolamwini, J., & Gebru, T. (2018). Gender Shades: Intersectional Accuracy Disparities in Commercial Gender Classification. *Proceedings of the 1st Conference on Fairness, Accountability and Transparency*, 81, 77–91. https://doi.org/10.48550/arXiv.1801.00001 (Last access: 10.08.2025).

When used properly, these technologies can help law enforcement reduce response times and improve investigative accuracy. However, their deployment must be governed by strict legal and ethical frameworks, ensuring:

- Compliance with data protection laws (e.g., GDPR);
- Transparency in system design and operation;
- Human oversight in decision-making processes;
- Mechanisms to minimize algorithmic bias and prevent discrimination.

2.2. Predictive Policing Methods

One of the most controversial applications of artificial intelligence in law enforcement is predictive policing — a strategy aimed at identifying crimes or potential offenders before a criminal act occurs. This approach relies on statistical analysis, historical data, machine learning, and algorithms designed to predict where, when, and by whom a crime is likely to happen.

The concept of predictive policing originated from the CompStat system, implemented by the New York Police Department in the 1990s. Its initial goal was to map crime incidents geographically and allocate police resources to so-called "hot spots,".[38] With advances in technology, predictive analysis has evolved beyond traditional statistics and has become data-driven algorithmic systems. Today, two primary models are commonly used:

- Place-based prediction – identifies *where* a crime is likely to occur;
- Person-based prediction – assesses *who* poses a high risk of committing or reoffending.

In this context, one of the most well-known systems was PredPol (Predictive Policing), initially developed by the Los Angeles Police Department (LAPD) in 2011. When processing information, PredPol relied on three key parameters:

- Type of crime
- Location coordinates

[38] Bratton, W. J., & Malinowski, S. W. (2008). Police Performance Management in Practice: Taking COMPSTAT to the Next Level. *Policing: A Journal of Policy and Practice, 2*(3), 259–265. https://doi.org/10.1093/police/pan040 (Last access: 10.08.2025).

- Time of the offense

The system provided police patrol units with a map indicating potential crime hotspots expected to emerge within the next few hours.[39]

In 2013, PredPol was tested in the United Kingdom, but its implementation was later suspended due to insufficient effectiveness and public criticism. The public expressed concern that the algorithm generated so-called "crime maps" without considering social context factors, which led to disproportionate targeting of low-income neighborhoods (BBC, 2017).

Another example of the use of artificial intelligence in crime prediction is HunchLab — a predictive analytics system employed by police departments in several U.S. cities (e.g., Philadelphia, St. Louis). The system was designed to identify areas with the highest likelihood of criminal activity. It utilized a wide range of data sources, including:

- Socioeconomic data – such as population income, unemployment rate, and education level;
- School locations – since crime risk can sometimes increase within certain social environments;
- Statistics on gatherings and activities – for instance, how frequently protests, conflicts, or public events occur in a given area;
- Historical crime locations and types – to identify spatial and temporal patterns of past offenses.

Taken together, these data helped the system generate so-called "heat maps" — visual representations highlighting areas with a higher predicted likelihood of criminal activity. [40]

In 2012, the Chicago Police Department developed a so-called "Strategic Subjects List" of around 400 individuals believed to be at the highest risk of either committing a crime or becoming a crime victim. The algorithm considered factors such as prior arrests, criminal records of known associates, and other behavioral indicators.

[39] Mohler, G. O., Short, M. B., Brantingham, P. J., Schoenberg, F. P., & Tita, G. E. (2015). Randomized Controlled Field Trials of Predictive Policing. *Journal of the American Statistical Association, 110*(512), 1399–1411. https://doi.org/10.1080/01621459.2015.1077710 (last accessed 11.08.2025).

[40] Lum, K., & Isaac, W. (2016). To predict and serve? *Significance, 13*(5), 14–19. https://doi.org/10.1111/j.1740-9713.2016.00960.x (last accessed: 11.08.2025).

However, subsequent analyses revealed that the system was highly biased and failed to perform accurately, often reinforcing pre-existing patterns of surveillance and discrimination.[41]

Thus, predictive algorithms are based on historical police data, which often reflect existing patterns of microaggression and racial profiling. As a result, the system does not truly predict the *next crime* — instead, it predicts the *subsequent arrest*, thereby creating a self-reinforcing cycle that perpetuates bias and inequality within law enforcement practices.[42]

Another major weakness of such systems lies in the lack of transparency — their algorithms are often closed to public and legal scrutiny, which undermines the fundamental principles of due process. In some instances, these predictive models also increase the risk of unwarranted suspicion and expand police surveillance powers, thereby eroding public trust in law enforcement. The European Union's proposed Artificial Intelligence Act (AI Act) classifies predictive policing methods as belonging to the category of high-risk systems and requires strict safeguards, including:

- Human oversight,
- Transparency,
- Proper authorization and documentation,
- Independent auditing (European Commission, 2021).[43]

In 2023, amendments to the AI Act introduced an explicit ban on behavioral profiling of citizens solely to predict criminal risk, as such practices clearly violate fundamental human rights.

---

[41] Saunders, J., Hunt, P., & Hollywood, J. S. (2016). Predictions put into practice: a quasi-experimental evaluation of Chicago's predictive policing pilot. *Journal of Experimental Criminology, 12*(3), 347–371. https://doi.org/10.1007/s11292-016-9272-0 (last accessed: 11.08.2025).

[42] Richardson, R., Schultz, J. M., & Crawford, K. (2019). Dirty data, bad predictions: How civil rights violations impact police data, predictive policing systems, and justice. *New York University Law Review, 94*, 192–233.

43 European Commission. (2021). Proposal for a Regulation of the European Parliament and of the Council Laying Down Harmonised Rules on Artificial Intelligence (Artificial Intelligence Act). https://eur-lex.europa.eu/legal-content/EN/TXT/?uri=CELEX:52021PC0206 (last accessed: 11.08.2025)

2.3. Automated Evidence Analysis

In modern criminal investigations, the volume and diversity of digital evidence are increasing so rapidly that traditional forensic methods often fail to ensure their complete and timely analysis. The integration of artificial intelligence into digital forensics enables the automated collection, analysis, and interpretation of data with minimal human intervention, significantly reducing both time and financial resources.[44]

For the automated analysis of digital evidence, specialized software platforms are widely used, such as Amped FIVE (for image restoration and video enhancement), Griffeye Analyze DI (for categorizing images and videos, including the detection of child exploitation cases), and Palantir Gotham (for link analysis and cross-referencing data from multiple sources). These tools have demonstrated high efficiency in cases where the volume of evidence exceeded tens of thousands of files.[45] For example, in the United States, in 2023, the California police used a machine learning–based system in a large-scale fraud case that analyzed 1.2 million emails within 48 hours, identified a network of fake invoices, and enabled the submission of this evidence for judicial proceedings.[46] In Estonia, a specialized platform implemented by the National Cybersecurity Center, which utilizes OSINT and network analysis modules, uncovered an international phishing network in 2022. The automation of analytical processes enabled investigators to respond within 72 hours, whereas using traditional methods, the same process would have taken several weeks.[47] In China, within the framework of the "Smart Court" project, automated digital evidence verification algorithms detected signs of deepfake manipulation in video evidence. This development proved particularly significant for ensuring the authenticity and integrity of evidence.[48]

Despite technological progress, the automatic analysis of digital evidence raises serious legal and ethical concerns. One of the central issues is the integrity of the chain

---

[44] Tivari, V., Dasari, V. S. R., & Wang, J. (2025). Digital Forensics in the Age of Large Language Models. *arXiv*. https://arxiv.org/abs/2504.02963 (last access: 11.08.2025).

[45] Billah, M. (2025). Developing an Explainable AI System for Digital Forensics: Enhancing Trust and Transparency in Flagging Events for Legal Evidence. *Journal of Forensic Science Research*, 9(2), 109–116. https://doi.org/10.29328/journal.jfsr.1001089 (last access: 11.08.2025).

[46] Johnson, L., & Patel, R. (2024). Machine Learning in Large-Scale Financial Crime Investigations. *International Journal of Digital Evidence*, 5(1), 45–63.

[47] Kõiv, M., & Laanemets, J. (2023). AI-Driven OSINT in Cybercrime Investigations: The Estonian Experience. *Baltic Journal of Law & Technology*, 12(3), 201–219.

[48] Zhang, Y. (2024). Deepfake Detection in Smart Court Systems: Challenges and Solutions. *China Law & Technology Review*, 8(2), 77–94.

of custody, the violation of which may render evidence inadmissible in court. Moreover, the "black box" nature of artificial intelligence systems creates significant transparency challenges — the parties involved in judicial proceedings may not have access to the reasoning or internal mechanisms behind an algorithm's specific conclusion.[49]

Ultimately, the automatic analysis of digital evidence in criminal law represents both an opportunity and a challenge: when properly implemented and regulated, it can significantly enhance the efficiency of investigations, yet it requires strict legal frameworks, algorithmic transparency, and adherence to the principle of human oversight.

2.4. Behavioral Analysis and Criminal Profiling

Behavioral analysis and criminal profiling are investigative methods based on the detailed study of an offender's behavioral patterns, motives, psychological traits, and the circumstances of the offense. Traditionally, this process relied heavily on the expertise of seasoned investigators and criminal psychologists; however, over the past decade, artificial intelligence (AI) and machine learning (ML) have significantly expanded their capabilities.[50]

Artificial intelligence systems that employ pattern recognition, network analysis, and natural language processing (NLP) algorithms now encompass stages of behavioral analysis that were once solely the domain of human intuition and experience. For instance, the automated analysis of textual communication and social media content allows investigators to identify a potential suspect's psychological profile even at the early stages of an investigation.[51]

In 2023, the Federal Bureau of Investigation (FBI) in the United States implemented an AI-based Behavioral Threat Assessment system that successfully prevented a planned school shooting by analyzing social media posts and online

[49] Wexler, R. (2021). Transparency in Algorithmic Criminal Evidence Analysis. *Yale Law Journal Forum*, 130, 221–240.

[50] Salfati, C. G., Horning, A., & Sorochinski, M. (2022). Behavioral Crime Linkage and Offender Profiling: Integrating AI Technologies. *Police Practice and Research*, 23(5), 512–529.

[51] Fitzgerald, J., & Winters, C. (2021). Natural Language Processing in Criminal Profiling: Opportunities and Risks. *Journal of Investigative Psychology and Offender Profiling*, 18(3), 245–263. https://doi.org/10.1002/jip.1608 (last access: 11.08.2025).

behavioral data. The system employed natural language processing (NLP) algorithms designed to detect patterns of aggressive behavior and hate speech.[52]

In 2022, the Metropolitan Police in the United Kingdom utilized behavioral analysis algorithms in a series of serial burglary investigations. The AI system processed over 15,000 surveillance camera recordings and identified the offender's unique gait and behavioral patterns, which significantly accelerated the identification and apprehension process.[53]

The Tokyo Metropolitan Police implemented a criminal profiling model that analyzes past homicide cases to generate a suspect's probable psychological and demographic profile. In 2024, the system successfully identified an offender based solely on crime scene photographs and descriptions of the evidence.[54]

The automation of behavioral analysis has raised numerous legal and ethical concerns. One of the primary risks is algorithmic bias, which can arise from imbalanced or unrepresentative datasets. This poses a danger of generating false positives or false negatives, potentially leading to the erroneous inclusion of innocent individuals in criminal investigations. Furthermore, the use of AI-based profiling is closely linked to issues of personal data protection, particularly when the analysis involves social media content or private communications.[55]

Ultimately, the role of artificial intelligence in behavioral analysis and criminal profiling can be a valuable investigative tool. Still, its application must rest on clear legal frameworks, appropriate oversight, and robust transparency mechanisms. These safeguards are essential to prevent legal violations and to mitigate potential societal risks associated with the misuse or overreach of such technologies.

---

[52] Thomas, E., Miller, J., & Chen, L. (2023). AI in Threat Assessment: Preventing Mass Violence Through Behavioral Analysis. *Journal of Law and Technology*, 15(2), 89–115.

[53] Henderson, P. (2022). Machine Learning Applications in Behavioral Crime Analysis: The UK Experience. *Policing: A Journal of Policy and Practice*, 16(4), 987–1004.

[54] Matsumoto, R. (2024). AI-Driven Criminal Profiling in Homicide Investigations: A Japanese Perspective. *Asian Journal of Criminology*, 19(1), 55–73.

[55] Oswald, M. (2021). Algorithmic Risk Assessment and the Right to a Fair Trial. *Criminal Law Review*, 6, 455–472.

2.5. Analysis of Big Data and Open-Source Intelligence (OSINT) in Combating Crime

In modern criminal investigation practices, Big Data and Open-Source Intelligence (OSINT) play a crucial role, enabling law enforcement agencies to utilize both publicly available and non-public large-scale datasets to enhance crime prevention and investigative efficiency. Big Data refers to the collection and analysis of massive, diverse, and high-velocity datasets, while OSINT involves gathering information from publicly accessible sources such as social media platforms, blogs, websites, satellite imagery, and online registries. These tools collectively allow investigators to identify hidden connections, detect emerging threats, and generate actionable intelligence in real time.[56]

The use of artificial intelligence in this field enables automatic integration, filtering, and analysis of data from various sources. Machine learning algorithms can identify connections, geographical trends, and temporal correlations, which is particularly valuable in the fight against organized crime and terrorism. Through advanced pattern recognition and predictive analytics, AI enables investigators to uncover networks and activities that would otherwise remain hidden within vast and complex datasets.[57] For example, in 2023, the New York Police Department (NYPD) implemented an OSINT platform that utilized Big Data analytics to identify violent groups on social media. The algorithm analyzed over three million posts and identified indicators of planned criminal activity, enabling authorities to prevent several attacks before they occurred.[58] In 2022, law enforcement authorities in Estonia used OSINT tools to uncover an international cyber fraud network, leading to a joint operation involving agencies from 12 countries. The AI-powered system enabled automatic translation and semantic analysis of data across multiple languages, enabling investigators to coordinate and efficiently interpret cross-border intelligence.[59] In 2024, the UK National Crime Agency (NCA) utilized Big Data analytics to uncover human trafficking routes by integrating satellite imagery with border control data. This

---

[56] Ridley, M., Young, M., & Taylor, R. (2022). Publicly Available Information in Criminal Investigations: OSINT Perspectives. *Police Practice and Research*, 23(4), 367–384.

[57] Hassani, H., Huang, X., & Silva, E. (2020). Digitalisation and Big Data in Criminal Justice. *Applied Economics*, 52(14), 1514–1528.

[58] Johnson, R., & Miller, T. (2023). OSINT and Big Data Analytics in Urban Policing. *Journal of Law Enforcement Technology*, 8(2), 201–218.

[59] Kõiv, M., & Laanemets, J. (2022). Integrating OSINT Tools for Transnational Cybercrime Investigations. *Baltic Journal of Law & Technology*, 11(4), 255–272.

advanced analytical approach enabled authorities to identify trafficking patterns in real time and ultimately rescue around 40 victims from exploitation.[60]

Despite these successful practical examples, the use of Big Data and Open-Source Intelligence (OSINT) in criminal investigations raises several legal and ethical challenges. In particular, there is a high risk of violations of personal data protection laws, mainly when information is obtained from closed or private social media profiles. Moreover, ensuring algorithmic transparency and independent oversight is essential to reduce the risks of data distortion, misuse, and incorrect interpretation during analysis.[61]

2.6. Ethical and Legal Challenges (Selective Bias, Human Rights, Data Protection)

The integration of artificial intelligence into criminal investigations, despite its significant benefits, raises serious ethical and legal challenges. These challenges are often linked to three main areas: selective bias, the protection of human rights, and the safeguarding of personal data.

Artificial intelligence systems are trained on data that may historically contain structural biases. If these biases are not identified and corrected, they can be reproduced or even amplified through algorithmic predictions.[62] For example, a 2020 study revealed that specific predictive policing systems used in major U.S. cities disproportionately focused on ethnic minorities, leading to unfair and discriminatory law enforcement practices.[63] The use of artificial intelligence in criminal law directly affects fundamental human rights principles, including the presumption of innocence, the right to a fair trial, and the right to privacy. For instance, the use of facial recognition technologies has sparked significant debate within the European Union, leading to the introduction of strict regulations on real-time biometric surveillance

[60] Williams, J. (2024). Satellite Imagery and Big Data in Anti-Trafficking Operations. *British Journal of Criminology*, 64(2), 215–233.

[61] Pauwels, L., Kindt, E., & Ponsaers, P. (2022). Ethical Challenges in Big Data Policing: Transparency and Accountability. *Policing and Society*, 32(5), 593–610.

[62] Barocas, S., Hardt, M., & Narayanan, A. (2023). *Fairness and Machine Learning*. MIT Press.

[63] Lum, K., & Isaac, W. (2021). To Predict and Serve? Predictive Policing and Civil Rights. *Annual Review of Law and Social Science*, 17, 253–271.

under the EU Artificial Intelligence Act (AI Act) in 2023.[64] These measures aim to ensure that technology does not undermine the protection of individual rights. Data protection is critical, particularly in criminal investigations where both public and confidential data are used. The EU General Data Protection Regulation (GDPR) establishes strict requirements regarding the lawfulness, purpose limitation, and data minimization of data processing.[65] In the use of artificial intelligence systems, the principle of human oversight (human-in-the-loop) is particularly important, ensuring that qualified professionals make final decisions while the algorithm serves only as a supporting tool. These types of risks and challenges have led to the suspension of several projects. For example, in 2020, a court in the Netherlands halted the SyRI system (an AI-based social risk indicator) due to human rights violations, as it lacked adequate oversight and failed to provide transparency to citizens.[66] In the United States, the COMPAS risk assessment system sparked legal disputes because its algorithmic outcomes were opaque and based on limited, biased data.[67] In 2024, law enforcement agencies revised the regulations governing the use of artificial intelligence systems, requiring annual independent audits to assess bias and data security compliance.

The tightening of ethical and legal frameworks is a necessary precondition for ensuring that the use of artificial intelligence in criminal investigations remains legally justified and socially acceptable. It is essential to conduct regular algorithmic audits, enforce strict data protection policies, and prioritize human rights alongside technological progress.

---

[64] European Parliament. (2023). *Artificial Intelligence Act.* https://eur-lex.europa.eu (Last access: 25.08.2025).

[65] Voigt, P., & Von dem Bussche, A. (2021). *The EU General Data Protection Regulation (GDPR): A Practical Guide.* Springer.

[66] Hert, P., & Papakonstantinou, V. (2021). The GDPR and Artificial Intelligence: Law and Ethics in the Digital Age. *Computer Law & Security Review*, 41, 105531.

[67] Angwin, J., Larson, J., Mattu, S., & Kirchner, L. (2016). Machine Bias. *ProPublica.* https://www.propublica.org/article/machine-bias-risk-assessments-in-criminal-sentencing (last access: 20.08.2025)

Chapter III. Artificial Intelligence in Criminal Proceedings

3.1. Attempts to Automate Judicial Decision-Making

The automation of judicial decision-making is one of the most controversial applications of artificial intelligence, around which debates still persist today. One of the primary objectives of integrating AI into judicial proceedings is to increase procedural efficiency, reduce time and costs, and, in some cases, minimize human bias.[68] However, this process is accompanied by significant technological, legal, and ethical challenges. Specific steps have already been taken in this direction. For instance, since 2019, the Estonian Ministry of Justice has launched a pilot project known as the "Robot Judge," designed to adjudicate small civil claims (up to €7,000) based on submitted evidence and pre-defined legal rules.[69] Since 2017, China has implemented the Smart Court initiative, which uses artificial intelligence systems to automatically categorize cases, generate preliminary decisions, and draft legal conclusions.[70] The system is particularly widely used in disputes related to intellectual property and online commerce. In several U.S. states, algorithmic platforms have been tested to assist judges in making bail or detention decisions using risk assessment tools.[71]

The main advantage of automation lies in standardized processes and more efficient decision-making. For example, China's *Smart Courts* have reduced the average duration of small claims proceedings by approximately 30%.[72]

---

[68] Surden, H. (2020). Artificial Intelligence and Law: An Overview. *Georgia State University Law Review*, 36(5), 1305–1338.

[69] Mak, V. (2021). The Impact of Artificial Intelligence on Judicial Decision-Making in Civil Law. *Netherlands Journal of Legal Philosophy*, 50(1), 3–22.

[70] Luo, J., Zhang, Y., & Li, M. (2022). Smart Courts and Judicial Efficiency in China: Empirical Evidence and Future Prospects. *International Journal of Law and Information Technology*, 30(3), 203–22

[71] Stevenson, M. T., & Doleac, J. L. (2021). Algorithmic risk assessment in the hands of humans. *The Journal of Law, Economics, & Organization*, 37(3), 579–607.

[72] Luo, J., Zhang, Y., & Li, M. (2022). Smart Courts and Judicial Efficiency in China: Empirical Evidence and Future Prospects. *International Journal of Law and Information Technology*, 30(3), 203–22

However, several significant challenges remain:

- Algorithmic transparency – the basis of a judicial decision must be understandable and explainable so that the parties can effectively exercise their right to appeal.[73]
- Human rights – automation must not conflict with the principle of a fair trial, as guaranteed by international legal instruments, including the European Convention on Human Rights.[74]
- Risk of bias – the algorithm may reflect unequal patterns present in historical data and thereby reinforce existing biases.[75]

3.2. Artificial Intelligence as a Supporting Tool for Judges

The use of artificial intelligence in the judicial system is not limited to decision automation. In many countries, AI is increasingly used as a support mechanism, providing judges with additional analytical resources, simplifying the processing of evidence, and enhancing procedural efficiency. This approach does not replace human judgment but complements it with technological assistance, allowing judges to make more informed and consistent decisions while maintaining control over the reasoning and outcomes of each case.[76]

Estonia is one of the pioneer countries in the field of judicial digitalization. In 2019, the country's Ministry of Justice launched a pilot project to introduce the "Robot Judge" platform for resolving small-claims cases (up to €7,000).[77] The system operates so that the parties submit their documents and evidence online, while the algorithm generates a draft decision based on predefined legal rules. Although a human judge

---

[73] Burrell, J. (2016). How the machine 'thinks': Understanding opacity in machine learning algorithms. *Big Data & Society*, 3(1), 1–12. https://doi.org/10.1177/2053951715622512 (Last access: 25.08.2025).

[74] European Court of Human Rights. (2023). *Guide on Article 6 of the European Convention on Human Rights*. https://echr.coe.int

[75] Barocas, S., Hardt, M., & Narayanan, A. (2023). *Fairness and Machine Learning*. MIT Press.

[76] Surden, H. (2020). Artificial Intelligence and Law: An Overview. *Georgia State University Law Review*, 36(5), 1305–1338.

[77] Mak, V. (2021). The Impact of Artificial Intelligence on Judicial Decision-Making in Civil Law. *Netherlands Journal of Legal Philosophy*, 50(1), 3–22.

still confirms the final judgment, the technology has significantly reduced processing time and administrative costs.

China's "Smart Court" initiative, launched in 2017, encompasses a comprehensive system designed to assist judges with case management and decision-making.[78]

The platform utilizes:

- Identification of similar cases – the algorithm locates previously adjudicated cases with comparable facts and provides relevant precedents to the judge;
- Automatic verification of evidence – the system checks whether the evidence has been obtained lawfully;
- Preliminary decision generation – the judge receives a draft judgment, which can then be reviewed and modified as needed.

According to data from the Supreme People's Court of China, the implementation of the "Smart Court" system has reduced case processing time by an average of 30% and increased the consistency of judicial decisions.[79]

The use of AI as an assistive tool in the judiciary offers several significant advantages:

- Simplification of judges' workload and reduction of caseload pressure;
- Increased consistency in judicial decisions;
- Enhanced transparency of judicial processes.

However, there are also important limitations, including:

- The risk of overreliance on technology;
- Lack of algorithmic transparency and the possibility of bias;
- Legal responsibility issues, especially when AI-generated recommendations prove inaccurate.

---

[78] Luo, J., Zhang, Y., & Li, M. (2022). Smart Courts and Judicial Efficiency in China: Empirical Evidence and Future Prospects. *International Journal of Law and Information Technology*, 30(3), 203–225.

[79] Supreme People's Court of China. (2023). *Annual Report on the Application of Artificial Intelligence in Courts*. Beijing: SPC Press.

International practice demonstrates that the most effective approach to integrating AI into judicial work is a hybrid model, in which technology performs analytical and support functions while final decisions remain in human hands. This model is particularly essential for ensuring legal certainty and safeguarding the principles of fair trial and judicial independence.

3.3. Algorithmic Models for the Evaluation of Evidence

Algorithmic models for evidence evaluation are a branch of artificial intelligence that analyzes the reliability, relevance, and credibility of evidence presented in court proceedings using predefined criteria and statistical methods.[80] Such models can be applied in both criminal and civil cases, though their role is particularly significant in cases involving large volumes of digital or physical evidence.

Algorithmic models operate through a specific framework and typically employ the following components:

- Bayesian theory or other statistical models to determine the probative value (weight) of evidence;[81]
- Neural networks that are trained on past cases to identify correlations among pieces of evidence;
- Text analysis tools that examine witness statements, expert opinions, and other documentary materials.

In the United Kingdom, the EVA (Evidence Evaluation Assistant) project was launched in 2021, utilizing Bayesian networks to assess evidence in criminal cases. The system evaluates both direct and circumstantial evidence, providing judges with a visual representation of the interconnections among evidence.[82] In the United States, algorithmic platforms have been tested at the federal level to examine digital evidence (e.g., electronic correspondence, GPS data) and assess its reliability based on data

---

[80] Bench-Capon, T., & Atkinson, K. (2021). Argumentation in Artificial Intelligence and Law. *Artificial Intelligence*, 296, 103506.

[81] Fenton, N., & Neil, M. (2019). Risk Assessment and Decision Analysis with Bayesian Networks. CRC Press.

[82] Fenton, N., Neil, M., & Berger, D. (2021). Bayesian Networks for Evaluating Legal Evidence. *Artificial Intelligence and Law*, 29(2), 167–187.

integrity and source validation.[83] In 2020, in a criminal case in the state of Maryland (State v. Johnson), the defense requested the use of an algorithmic evidence-evaluation model — the Bayesian Network Evidence Evaluator — to assess the credibility of a witness's testimony. The system, developed by a team of experts from George Mason University, was based on the coordinated analysis of witness statements and physical evidence. The algorithm demonstrated that the credibility of the witness's testimony was significantly reduced due to unavoidable inconsistencies identified when compared with the physical evidence.[84] The judge did not treat the algorithmic output as independent evidence, but noted that the model's analysis helped in understanding the interrelation of the evidence. Ultimately, this assessment was used as an additional argument in delivering an acquittal verdict. This case clearly illustrates that algorithmic models cannot yet replace a judge's final decision, but they can significantly impact the evaluation of evidence and simplify the interpretation of complex factual circumstances.

Under the KEI Program in the Netherlands, several AI-based systems assist judges and prosecutors by structuring evidence and identifying contradictions across different sources.

The main advantages of these models include rapid, structured analysis of large volumes of data, which significantly reduces the time judges and legal parties spend. Moreover, these tools can minimize human error and strengthen the logical consistency of arguments.

However, several issues remain:

- Transparency – The algorithmic evaluation process is often complicated to explain, making it challenging to appeal its outcomes.
- Bias risk – If the model is trained on biased data, its assessments may also be biased.
- Legal status – Many jurisdictions have yet to define how algorithmic analysis results should be evaluated in court.

In the future, algorithmic models for evidence evaluation may become an important support tool in judicial proceedings. However, their use must remain

[83] Casey, E., Ferraro, M., & Nguyen, L. (2022). Digital Evidence in the Courtroom: AI-based Assessment and Admissibility. *Digital Investigation*, 40, 301–315.

[84] Casey, E., Ferraro, M., & Nguyen, L. (2022). Digital Evidence in the Courtroom: AI-based Assessment and Admissibility. *Digital Investigation*, 40, 301–315.

transparent, supervised, and aligned with human rights protection principles. The best practice is a hybrid approach, where AI provides analytical support but a human judge makes the final decision.

3.4. Risk Assessment Systems

Risk assessment systems are algorithmic tools designed to assist courts and law enforcement agencies in determining the likelihood that a defendant may commit a new offense, abscond, or pose other risks. These models are based on statistical data and/or machine learning methods, utilizing a range of demographic, social, criminal, and behavioral variables related to the individual being assessed.[85]

COMPAS (Correctional Offender Management Profiling for Alternative Sanctions) is a widely used algorithm in the United States that supports decision-making in pretrial detention, probation, and supervision. The system evaluates multiple criteria — such as prior criminal history, social connections, substance use, and psychological assessments — and assigns a numerical score reflecting the defendant's overall "risk level,".[86]

The Public Safety Assessment (PSA) model, also used in the United States and developed by the Laura and John Arnold Foundation, takes a different approach. This model relies solely on objective data, such as prior offenses and court appearance history, and does not require subjective interviews. Its main goal is to reduce bias and enhance transparency in the risk assessment process.[87] In the United Kingdom, the OASys (Offender Assessment System) operates as a comprehensive framework that not only assesses the risk of reoffending but also identifies the rehabilitative needs of offenders. Using this system, probation services and prison administrations develop individualized management and rehabilitation plans, making OASys a valuable tool

---

[85] Berk, R. (2019). Accuracy and fairness for juvenile justice risk assessments. *Journal of Empirical Legal Studies*, 16(1), 175–194.

[86] Angwin, J., Larson, J., Mattu, S., & Kirchner, L. (2016). Machine bias: There's software used across the country to predict future criminals. *ProPublica*. https://www.propublica.org/article/machine-bias-risk-assessments-in-criminal-sentencing (Last access: 20.08.2025).

[87] Stevenson, M. T., & Doleac, J. L. (2021). Algorithmic risk assessment in the hands of humans. *The Journal of Law, Economics, & Organization*, 37(3), 579–607.

not only for supervision and control but also for offender reform and reintegration.[88] In Canada, the LSI-R (Level of Service Inventory–Revised) is widely used. This system evaluates an offender's social environment, education, employment status, and attitudes based on 54 indicators. It is particularly useful for monitoring individuals on probation, as it tracks not only risk levels but also the progress of rehabilitation, providing a structured, evidence-based framework for offender management.

It is evident that risk assessment systems offer numerous benefits. Among these are efficient resource allocation and use, reduced pretrial detention rates for low-risk individuals, and increased data-driven, objective decision-making.

However, these systems also present many significant challenges, including:

- Risk of bias — A well-known example is ProPublica's 2016 investigation, which showed that COMPAS assigned higher risk scores to African American defendants regardless of actual outcomes.[89]
- Lack of transparency — Many commercial algorithms are proprietary, making it difficult to examine how they operate internally.
- Human rights concerns — Under international standards, decisions based on algorithmic assessments must be appealable and fully explainable.

3.5. Standardization of Court Proceedings and Time Efficiency

The implementation of artificial intelligence (AI) technologies in judicial proceedings holds significant potential to standardize processes and improve efficiency. Standardization involves organizing the stages, procedures, and documentation of court proceedings into a uniform, predefined structure, thereby reducing procedural errors, accelerating case management, and increasing transparency of the process.[90]

---

[88] Howard, P., & Dixon, L. (2019). The construction and validation of OASys. *Criminal Behaviour and Mental Health*, 29(1), 32–47.

[89] Angwin, J., Larson, J., Mattu, S., & Kirchner, L. (2016). Machine bias: There's software used across the country to predict future criminals. *ProPublica*. https://www.propublica.org/article/machine-bias-risk-assessments-in-criminal-sentencing (Last access: 20.08.2025).

[90] Susskind, R. (2019). *Online courts and the future of justice*. Oxford University Press.

Artificial intelligence (AI) systems—particularly platforms based on natural language processing (NLP) and machine learning—can automatically format and complete legal documents, create standardized checklists for preliminary case review, and monitor procedural deadlines. For example, in Singapore, the Litigation System ensures a standardized format for all court documents. It automatically verifies their procedural compliance before submission, thereby reducing instances of process delays caused by technical errors.[91]

The use of artificial intelligence also significantly reduces the duration of judicial proceedings. For instance, within the Estonian Smart Court System concept, AI performs automatic classification and preliminary legal assessment of documents related to small claims, leaving the judge responsible only for the substantive stage of the hearing.[92] This approach reduces the average case processing time from several months to just a few weeks.

In several U.S. states, AI-based case management systems are in operation. These systems automatically schedule court hearings, account for the parties' availability, and reduce the risk of procedural delays. According to studies, the use of such systems has shortened the average case completion time by 20–25%.[93]

Despite the apparent benefits, standardizing proceedings and improving time efficiency through artificial intelligence come with specific challenges. These include:

- Risk of losing procedural flexibility – when all cases are confined within a uniform template;
- Risks of technical failures and cybersecurity threats;
- Data protection requirements – especially in the context of the automated processing of personal and confidential information.

The standardization of judicial processes and the improvement of time efficiency through artificial intelligence can be achieved from both technical and organizational perspectives. However, successful implementation requires a legally sound framework,

---

[91] Ng, M. (2021). Digital transformation in Singapore's judiciary: The eLitigation experience. *Asian Journal of Law and Society*, 8(1), 87–104.

[92] European Union. (2023). *Algorithms, rule of law, and the future of justice*. Publications Office of the European Union. https://op.europa.eu/en/publication-detail/-/publication/f0a5abdd-7d32-11ee-99ba-01aa75ed71a1/language-en (last access: 20.08.2025 წ.).

[93] McMillan, J. (2022). Artificial intelligence in court case management: Efficiency and fairness. *Journal of Law and Technology*, 18(2), 45–67.

robust data security mechanisms, and sufficient flexibility to enable the system to adapt to the specific requirements of each case.

3.6. Challenges to the Fairness and Transparency of Judicial Procedures

The integration of artificial intelligence into criminal proceedings extends beyond technical and organizational benefits; it also raises significant legal, ethical, and societal challenges. Ensuring fairness and transparency in the process is particularly crucial, as the role of the judiciary extends beyond achieving a legal outcome to maintaining public trust in the justice system.[94]

The fairness of judicial procedures is based on fundamental principles such as the presumption of innocence, equality of the parties, and the protection of the legal guarantees of all participants in the process. The use of artificial intelligence in this context raises important questions, such as:

- Can algorithmic decisions be biased due to prejudiced or unbalanced data?
- How can the parties examine and appeal an algorithmic conclusion if its internal logic is confidential or difficult to understand?

According to research, the risk of bias in algorithmic decision-making is particularly high when algorithms are trained on so-called historical data, which may already contain systemic inequalities.[95]

The transparency of algorithmic functioning in judicial proceedings is a matter of critical importance. Systems developed by commercial companies often operate as so-called "black boxes," meaning that their logic and decision-making processes are not publicly accessible.

[94] Byrnes, M. (2021). Artificial intelligence and procedural fairness in courts. *Judicial Review*, 26(3), 255–272.

[95] Richardson, R., Schultz, J., & Crawford, K. (2019). Dirty data, bad predictions: How civil rights violations impact police data, predictive policing systems, and justice. *New York University Law Review Online*, 94, 15–55.

This complicates:

- The ability of the parties to challenge the decision;
- The ability of the judge to verify the system's accuracy and fairness.

At the international level, for example, the European Union's Artificial Intelligence Act (AI Act) requires developers of high-risk systems to ensure the explainability of algorithms. This provision directly applies to technologies used within judicial systems.[96]

A 2016 investigation by ProPublica revealed that the U.S. risk assessment system COMPAS often assigned higher risk scores to African American defendants compared to white defendants, highlighting the problem of replicating historical bias within algorithmic decision-making.[97]

China's "Smart Court" model, despite its success in improving procedural efficiency, has faced criticism for the potential misuse of centralized data and automated decision-making to exert political influence or control.[98]

To safeguard fairness and transparency, it is essential to:

1. Establish minimum standards for algorithmic explainability;
2. Create independent oversight mechanisms;
3. Implement regular bias assessments and corrective procedures.

The integration of artificial intelligence into the judicial system must align with international standards and human rights protection principles, ensuring that the technology does not undermine the very values it is intended to promote and protect.

---

[96] European Commission. (2021). Proposal for a Regulation laying down harmonised rules on artificial intelligence (Artificial Intelligence Act). https://eur-lex.europa.eu/legal-content/EN/TXT/?uri=CELEX:52021PC0206

[97] Angwin, J., Larson, J., Mattu, S., & Kirchner, L. (2016). Machine bias: There's software used across the country to predict future criminals. *ProPublica.* https://www.propublica.org/article/machine-bias-risk-assessments-in-criminal-sentencing (last access: 15.08.2025).

[98] Liu, H. (2020). Smart courts in China: Opportunities and challenges. *Computer Law & Security Review*, 36, 105–127.

Chapter IV. Legal and Ethical Frameworks for the Use of Artificial Intelligence

4.1. European Regulations and the Criminal Law Context

The European Union's Artificial Intelligence Act (Regulation (EU) 2024/1689, effective from August 1, 2024) is the first horizontal regulation on artificial intelligence in Europe. It differentiates risks by use type into four categories: unacceptable, high, limited, and minimal.

In the context of criminal law, particular significance is attached to the "unacceptable risk" category, which prohibits practices such as predictive policing, social scoring systems, and biometric identification (including profiling individuals based on perceived criminal risk) when such applications are used without an explicit and legitimate connection to the underlying data or purpose.

"Predictive policing" refers to the use of algorithms and statistical models to forecast where or when a crime might occur, or who might commit one, often relying on historical data — such as records of past offenses, geographic patterns, or profiling information. Such systems are highly susceptible to algorithmic bias and discrimination, as they may reinforce existing inequalities or stereotypes. Moreover, predictive policing can violate the presumption of innocence and undermine judicial oversight, notably when the model lacks transparency and explainability.[99]

Article 5(1)(d) of the EU Artificial Intelligence Act explicitly prohibits such practices, stating that:

"The placing on the market, putting into service, or use of an artificial intelligence system for the purpose of assessing or predicting the risk of a natural person committing a criminal offense, solely based on profiling or assessment of that person's personality traits and characteristics, shall be prohibited."

However, this prohibition does not apply to AI systems used to support the assessment of an individual's potential involvement in criminal activity based on objective, verifiable facts directly related to the criminal conduct in question.

---

[99] European Law Blog. (2024). *Predictive policing in the AI Act: meaningful ban or paper tiger?*

The Act also prohibits law enforcement authorities from using real-time remote biometric identification systems in public spaces. The only exceptions allowed under the Act are narrowly defined cases, such as:

- the targeted search for missing persons;
- the prevention of a specific, serious, and imminent threat;
- The detection, localization, identification, or prosecution of a suspect involved in a serious criminal offense.

Equally noteworthy is the Dutch approach. The SyRI (System Risk Indication) was an algorithmic risk assessment system developed by the Dutch government to identify social risks, specifically aiming to detect fraud and violations of social welfare, tax, and labor legislation.

Its operational principle was as follows:

- Various state agencies — both central and local — shared extensive categories of data, including employment history, income, tax records, social welfare benefits, health information, and more.
- These datasets were consolidated and processed through an algorithmic model, which then identified individuals classified as "high-risk."
- The results were compiled into a "Risk Notification Registry," from which the relevant government agencies received the data for further investigation and response.[100]

On 5 February 2020, the District Court of The Hague ruled that the use of SyRI violated Article 8 of the European Convention on Human Rights (the right to respect for private life) and banned its further use in the Netherlands. Although the court acknowledged the government's argument that detecting social fraud served a "legitimate public interest," it found that the law failed to ensure a fair balance between the public goal and the restriction of individual rights. The judgment emphasized the rapid introduction of new technologies and the serious privacy threats arising from their misuse. The court particularly highlighted the lack of transparency in the SyRI system, which made judicial oversight difficult and limited individuals' ability to challenge or appeal the system's assessments. Furthermore, the court noted that SyRI

[100] Landmark judgment from the Netherlands on digital welfare states and human rights, Open Global Rights, Analyzing present and future of human rights, https://www.openglobalrights.org/landmark-judgment-from-netherlands-on-digital-welfare-states/ (Last access 20.08.2025).

was applied exclusively in so-called "problematic neighborhoods," creating a risk of discrimination and social stigmatization.[101]

This judgment represents one of the first legal precedents against digital social systems that infringe upon human rights, demonstrating how strategic litigation, advocacy, and international cooperation can lead to tangible legal and policy changes. It is also noteworthy that the court's reasoning in this decision closely aligns with the European concept discussed earlier regarding the restrictions on predictive policing — both emphasizing the protection of privacy, transparency, and proportionality in the use of artificial intelligence and algorithmic systems.[102]

The General Data Protection Regulation (GDPR, Regulation (EU) 2016/679) grants every individual the right to know how and why their personal data is being processed, while law enforcement authorities, under the Law Enforcement Directive, are obligated to structure their procedures effectively and purposefully to ensure data purpose limitation, confidentiality, and compliance with the principles of lawful processing.

The European Artificial Intelligence Act discussed above and the GDPR share the same fundamental objective and, in many respects, complement each other. The GDPR establishes the standards for the protection of personal data. At the same time, the EU Artificial Intelligence Act introduces additional layers of oversight and judicial or administrative control over the use of artificial intelligence — particularly in the criminal justice sector, where high-risk AI systems must operate under strict requirements of reliability, transparency, and human supervision.

4.2. The American Approach

The Constitution of the United States firmly guarantees the individual's right to be protected from arbitrary or disproportionate interference through the Due Process Clauses. Both the federal and state legal systems ensure that every person enjoys the right to a fair trial and the protection of fundamental human rights. The U.S.

---

101 Moynihan, C. (2020, February 10). Dutch Court Blocks Use of Algorithmic Risk Scoring System for Welfare Fraud Detection. ***Just Security***. Retrieved from https://www.justsecurity.org/68620/dutch-court-blocks-use-of-algorithmic-risk-scoring-system-for-welfare-fraud-detection/ (Last access: 15.08.2025)

102 Bundesverfassungsgericht, (2023) *Press release on Hesse/Hamburg automated police data analysis ruling*

Constitution also proclaims the principle of legal equality for all individuals, ensuring that no person shall be subjected to unfair or unreasonable discrimination. These principles form the cornerstone of American jurisprudence, upholding justice and the rule of law across the nation.[103]

Predictive policing presents a significant challenge to the principles above, because:

- Algorithms often rely on historical data that already contains racial or social bias;
- As a result, there is concern that such methods may increase the risk of discrimination in practice. In these cases, the law may function as a so-called "general law" that, in effect, produces or reinforces discriminatory outcomes, even if its text does not explicitly contain discriminatory provisions. Ultimately, this stands in direct conflict with the principles of equality and the prohibition of discrimination.[104] For example, if the law states that "all persons are prohibited from carrying cold weapons," this rule appears to apply equally to all citizens. However, if in practice — including through the operation of a specific system or algorithm — law enforcement authorities enforce this rule more strictly against a particular ethnic group, the law may, in effect, be considered discriminatory, even though its text does not explicitly single out that group.
- Risk assessment algorithms, such as the COMPAS program, may conflict with the constitutionally guaranteed principle of Equal Protection if their frameworks result in discrimination against specific groups and are not sufficiently narrowly tailored to achieve a legitimate governmental interest.[105]

In 2024, the U.S. Congress voiced criticism toward the Department of Justice (DOJ) for openly funding predictive policing projects, even though such programs are often characterized by racial bias and procedural deficiencies that ultimately violate human rights.[106]

---

[103] Tribe, L. H. (2000). *American constitutional law* (3rd ed.). Foundation Press. pp. 1335 ff

[104] O'Donnell, R. M. (2019). *Challenging racist predictive policing algorithms under the Equal Protection Clause* (NYU Law Review).

[105] Pre-crime and predictive policing: Legal and ethical considerations. (2025). *Morolawyers.com.*

[106] US lawmakers tell DOJ to quit blindly funding 'predictive' police tools. (2024, January).

4.3. Data Protection, the Need for Human Oversight, and Algorithmic Transparency

The protection of personal data is one of the central principles in the legal regulation of artificial intelligence. The General Data Protection Regulation (GDPR) establishes the core principles of data processing — lawfulness, transparency, purpose limitation, data minimization, accuracy, and security.[107] Data protection is particularly crucial in law enforcement, where sensitive categories of data — including biometric information — are frequently processed.[108] International instruments — such as the OECD Privacy Guidelines and the Council of Europe Convention[108] — obligate states and private-sector entities to protect personal data throughout the lifecycle of artificial intelligence systems. [109]

Human intervention is an essential safeguard to ensure that decisions based on artificial intelligence are not executed automatically and that errors can be prevented or corrected. The EU Artificial Intelligence Act requires that high-risk AI systems be designed in such a way that humans can intervene in key processes — including the suspension, modification, or review of the system's operation — particularly when such decisions affect an individual's rights and freedoms.[110] Such human intervention within the system must be ensured not only at the technical level, but also at the legal level.[111] In practice, this means that any decision made by the system must be verifiable, allowing a human to examine and understand the source and reasoning behind the decision.[112]

Algorithmic transparency means that the operation and decision-making processes of artificial intelligence systems must be described and communicated in a way that is understandable not only to developers but also to users and regulators. The EU General Data Protection Regulation (GDPR) directly addresses automated decision-making and establishes the "right to explanation." Accordingly, an individual must be able to obtain an explanation of why a particular automated decision was made about them.[113] Any decision made by an AI system must be explainable and

---

[107] Regulation (EU) 2016/679, General Data Protection Regulation, Art. 5

[108] Ibid., Art. 9(1) – Sensitive data categories, including biometric data.

[109] OECD. (2013). *OECD Guidelines on the Protection of Privacy and Transborder Flows of Personal Data.*

[110] Regulation (EU) 2024/1689, Artificial Intelligence Act, Art. 14 – Human oversight requirements

[111] OECD. (2019). *OECD Principles on Artificial Intelligence*, Principle 1.2.

[112] Floridi, L., & Cowls, J. (2019). *A Unified Framework of Five Principles for AI in Society*. Harvard Data Science Review, 1(1).

[113] GDPR, Art. 22 – Automated individual decision-making, including profiling.

interpretable — this is the key element that helps avoid the so-called "black box" effect mentioned earlier, ensuring transparency and accountability in the use of artificial intelligence.[114] In practice, this requires implementing technical methods to reconstruct the algorithm's behavior, such as logging, recording intermediate model states, and documenting the system's functioning.[115]

[114] High-Level Expert Group on AI. (2019). *Ethics Guidelines for Trustworthy AI*. European Commission.

[115] Doshi-Velez, F., & Kim, B. (2017). *Towards a Rigorous Science of Interpretable Machine Learning*. arXiv:1702.08608.

Chapter V. International Experience

5.1. International Practices: The United States, the United Kingdom, China, and Estonia

In the United States, one of the most critical considerations in the use of artificial intelligence is protecting the principle of equality and preventing discrimination. Since 2023, the regulation titled "Safe, Secure, and Trustworthy Development and Use of Artificial Intelligence" (Executive Order 14110) has been in force. This document establishes several conceptual requirements for the development and use of artificial intelligence, including:

- **Safety and Security:** The document establishes that artificial intelligence systems must be safe and secure. Achieving this goal requires robust, reliable, repeatable, and standardized evaluations of AI systems, along with the development of policies, institutional mechanisms, and, where necessary, additional tools to ensure testing, understanding, and mitigation of AI-related risks before deployment. This also includes managing the most critical safety risks associated with AI — including those related to biotechnology, cybersecurity, critical infrastructure, and national security threats — especially when AI systems operate in opaque or difficult-to-understand ways. Testing and evaluation, including post-deployment monitoring, help ensure that AI systems function as intended, are resilient to misuse or harmful alteration, are developed ethically, operate in secure environments, and comply with federal laws and policies. The President's Administration also promotes the creation of adequate mechanisms for labeling and content provenance, allowing Americans to distinguish when content has been generated using artificial intelligence and when it has not.[116]
- **Government Support and Fair Competition:** The document reaffirms the U.S. Administration's commitment to supporting projects focused on the application of artificial intelligence across diverse sectors. At the same time, it emphasizes the risks posed by dominant market positions held by certain

[116] Executive Order No. 14110, Safe, Secure, and Trustworthy Development and Use of Artificial Intelligence, 88 Fed. Reg. 75191 (Nov. 1, 2023). Retrieved from https://www.federalregister.gov/documents/2023/11/01/2023-24283/safe-secure-and-trustworthy-development-and-use-of-artificial-intelligence (Last access: 20.08.2025 წ.).

companies in the AI industry and highlights the need to preserve fair and open competition in this rapidly developing field.[117]

- **Labor Rights:** The document affirms that the responsible development and use of artificial intelligence must include a commitment to supporting American workers. As AI creates new jobs and industries, all employees must have the opportunity to participate—including through collective bargaining—so they can benefit from these emerging opportunities. According to the document, vocational training and education should be adapted to support a diverse workforce and ensure access to opportunities generated by AI technologies. The implementation of AI in the workplace must not occur in a way that violates workers' rights, diminishes job quality, encourages excessive employee surveillance, reduces market competition, creates new health and safety risks, or leads to harmful working conditions. The regulation stresses that the perspectives should inform the next critical steps in AI development of workers, unions, educators, and employers to promote the responsible use of AI—one that improves workers' lives, enhances human labor, and ensures that everyone can safely benefit from technological innovation and its opportunities.[118]
- **Equality and Civil Rights:** The document establishes that AI policy must align with the promotion of equality and civil rights. It explicitly prohibits the use of artificial intelligence in ways that worsen the conditions of individuals who already face unequal access to opportunity and justice. According to the document, the misuse of AI in employment, housing, and healthcare can deepen discrimination and bias rather than improve the quality of life. It cites examples where irresponsibly implemented AI systems have reinforced existing inequalities, created new discriminatory practices, and intensified both online and physical risks. The regulation requires that AI systems comply with federal laws, ensuring rigorous technical evaluations, careful oversight, consultation with affected communities, and strict regulatory measures. It further mandates that AI developers and deployers must adhere to standards that protect the

[117] Executive Order No. 14110, Safe, Secure, and Trustworthy Development and Use of Artificial Intelligence, 88 Fed. Reg. 75191 (Nov. 1, 2023). Retrieved from https://www.federalregister.gov/documents/2023/11/01/2023-24283/safe-secure-and-trustworthy-development-and-use-of-artificial-intelligence (Last access: 20.08.2025 წ.).

[118] Executive Order No. 14110, Safe, Secure, and Trustworthy Development and Use of Artificial Intelligence, 88 Fed. Reg. 75191 (Nov. 1, 2023). Retrieved from https://www.federalregister.gov/documents/2023/11/01/2023-24283/safe-secure-and-trustworthy-development-and-use-of-artificial-intelligence (Last access: 20.08.2025 წ.).

public from unlawful discrimination and abuse, including within the judicial system and federal institutions. Ultimately, these measures aim to safeguard civil rights, individual freedoms, equality, and justice in the age of artificial intelligence.[119]

- **Consumer Rights:** The document declares that the interests of Americans who use, interact with, or purchase AI-based products must be protected. The use of new technologies, including artificial intelligence, does not exempt organizations from their legal obligations, and consumer protection mechanisms are especially vital during periods of technological change.
  According to the document, the federal government will enforce existing consumer protection laws and principles and will implement safeguards to prevent fraud, unintentional bias, discrimination, privacy violations, and other harms. Such protection is particularly crucial in critical sectors — including healthcare, financial services, education, housing, law, and transportation — where AI errors or misuse can harm patients, consumers, or small businesses, or endanger their safety and rights. At the same time, the document encourages the responsible use of artificial intelligence to protect consumers, enhance the quality of goods and services, reduce costs, and expand choice and accessibility.[120]
- **Privacy and the Right to Private Life:** The document emphasizes that the privacy and civil liberties of Americans must be protected throughout the development and deployment of artificial intelligence. It notes that AI technologies facilitate the collection, re-identification, linking, inference, and use of sensitive information, thereby increasing the risk that personal data may be exploited or exposed. To mitigate this risk, the document directs the federal government to ensure that data collection, use, and storage are conducted lawfully, securely, and with safeguards to minimize privacy and personal life risks. It also requires that federal agencies employ available policy and

---

[119] Executive Order No. 14110, Safe, Secure, and Trustworthy Development and Use of Artificial Intelligence, 88 Fed. Reg. 75191 (Nov. 1, 2023). Retrieved from https://www.federalregister.gov/documents/2023/11/01/2023-24283/safe-secure-and-trustworthy-development-and-use-of-artificial-intelligence (Last access 20.08.2025 წ.).

[120] Executive Order No. 14110, Safe, Secure, and Trustworthy Development and Use of Artificial Intelligence, 88 Fed. Reg. 75191 (Nov. 1, 2023). Retrieved from https://www.federalregister.gov/documents/2023/11/01/2023-24283/safe-secure-and-trustworthy-development-and-use-of-artificial-intelligence (Last access: 20.08.2025).

technical tools, including privacy-enhancing technologies (PETs), when appropriate, to protect individual privacy and prevent legal and social harms.[121]

- **Federal Governance:** The document establishes that it is essential for the federal government to manage the risks arising from its use of artificial intelligence and to strengthen its internal capacity for the regulation, governance, and responsible application of AI in order to achieve better outcomes. According to the document, this effort begins with people — the nation's most valuable asset. It calls for measures to attract, retain, and develop AI professionals committed to public service, including individuals from underrepresented communities and across diverse disciplines such as technology, policy, management, procurement, regulation, ethics, governance, and law. Furthermore, the document instructs the federal government to ensure that all employees receive adequate training to understand the benefits, risks, and limitations of AI, to modernize IT infrastructure, eliminate bureaucratic barriers, and to guarantee the implementation and use of AI systems that are safe, ethical, and respectful of human rights.[122]
- **International Cooperation:** The document states that the federal government must lead in advancing global social, economic, and technological progress, just as the United States has done during previous eras of transformative innovation. This leadership is not defined solely by technological achievement, but also by the implementation of systems and safeguards necessary for the responsible use of technology, and by developing and promoting these frameworks in collaboration with other nations. The document directs the U.S. government to cooperate with international allies and partners to effectively manage AI-related risks, realize its positive potential, and develop unified approaches to shared global challenges. According to the document, the federal government will work with other countries to promote principles and practices of AI safety and security, and to serve as a leader in global dialogue and cooperation, ensuring that the benefits of artificial intelligence extend to the

[121] Executive Order No. 14110, Safe, Secure, and Trustworthy Development and Use of Artificial Intelligence, 88 Fed. Reg. 75191 (Nov. 1, 2023). Retrieved from https://www.federalregister.gov/documents/2023/11/01/2023-24283/safe-secure-and-trustworthy-development-and-use-of-artificial-intelligence (Last access: 20.08.2025).

[122] Executive Order No. 14110, Safe, Secure, and Trustworthy Development and Use of Artificial Intelligence, 88 Fed. Reg. 75191 (Nov. 1, 2023). Retrieved from https://www.federalregister.gov/documents/2023/11/01/2023-24283/safe-secure-and-trustworthy-development-and-use-of-artificial-intelligence (Last access: 20.08.2025).

entire world—without deepening inequality, harming human rights, or causing other forms of damage.[123]

At the local level in the United States, several cities have restricted or outright banned police use of facial recognition technology. The civil society sector has been actively advocating for such restrictions through movements like "ban-the-scan." However, in practice, secret applications and regulatory loopholes continue to emerge. For example, in 2025, cases such as New Orleans and the "Project NOLA" initiative revealed ongoing circumvention of established rules and the covert use of facial recognition systems, highlighting persistent challenges in enforcing transparency and accountability.[124]

In 2016, the Wisconsin Supreme Court reviewed the case of *State v. Loomis*, in which the COMPAS algorithm was used to assist in determining the defendant's pretrial detention and sentencing.[125] The defendant argued that the system lacked transparency and was potentially biased.[126] The court ultimately allowed the use of the system but emphasized that such algorithms should be treated only as auxiliary tools and not as decisive evidence in judicial decision-making.[127] Within the court's reasoning, this case became a precedent in the American legal system, shaping the national debate on the use of algorithmic tools in criminal justice.

In 2019, a legal dispute that began in Wales soon became one of the most significant precedents in the United Kingdom concerning privacy protection and the use of artificial intelligence. Edward Bridges, a Cardiff resident and civil rights activist, noticed that police were frequently deploying special cameras throughout the city that scanned passersby's faces in real time. These were not ordinary CCTV cameras—they used Live Facial Recognition (LFR) technology, which instantly compared scanned faces to a police "watchlist." If a match was detected, operators received an alert and could act immediately on-site.

---

[123] Executive Order No. 14110, Safe, Secure, and Trustworthy Development and Use of Artificial Intelligence, 88 Fed. Reg. 75191 (Nov. 1, 2023). Retrieved from https://www.federalregister.gov/documents/2023/11/01/2023-24283/safe-secure-and-trustworthy-development-and-use-of-artificial-intelligence (Last access: 20.08.2025 წ.).

[124] The Washington Post. (2025, May 19). *Police secretly monitored New Orleans with facial recognition.*

[125] *State v. Loomis*, 881 N.W.2d 749 (Wis. 2016).

[126] Angwin, J., Larson, J., Mattu, S., & Kirchner, L. (2016). *Machine Bias*. ProPublica.

[127] Ferguson, A. G. (2017). *The Rise of Big Data Policing*. NYU Press.

Bridges found himself captured by these cameras on multiple occasions — once during a mass protest and another time simply while shopping. He was neither a suspect nor involved in any legal proceedings, yet his facial data was processed and temporarily stored by the police. For him, this raised serious concerns that his right to privacy might have been violated. Consequently, he filed a lawsuit against the authorities in *Bridges v. South Wales Police*, arguing that his right to private life, data protection principles, and the principle of equality had been infringed — violations that contradicted both domestic law and internationally recognized fundamental rights.

Initially, the court ruled that the police actions were lawful, finding that the public safety purpose justified their use in proportion. However, Bridges appealed to the Court of Appeal, which overturned the decision in its entirety, finding that the police had no clear, predefined, and transparent rules governing who could be included on the watchlist or under what circumstances facial data could be processed.

Moreover, the police had failed to conduct a proper Data Protection Impact Assessment (DPIA) and did not implement bias testing, constituting a breach of the Equality Act. The court clarified that while facial recognition systems (LFR) are not inherently unlawful, their use in public spaces demands strict regulation, oversight, and accountability.

Ultimately, *Bridges v. South Wales Police* became a landmark precedent, demonstrating that even when advanced technology aims to enhance security, the processing of personal data must always be governed by clear, transparent rules — ensuring that civil liberties are not overstepped in the pursuit of safety.[128] In relation to European countries, the Artificial Intelligence Act discussed above establishes a unified legal framework that prohibits "unacceptable" practices, such as social scoring, real-time biometric identification in public spaces (with narrowly defined exceptions), and person-based predictive policing. It also imposes strict requirements on high-risk AI systems, particularly those used in sensitive contexts like law enforcement and justice. The General Data Protection Regulation (GDPR) remains the core European instrument for personal data protection, setting out general standards for lawful data processing — including Article 22, which specifically addresses automated decision-making and profiling.[129] —which also partially covers issues related to artificial intelligence. Under European approaches, the use of artificial intelligence in law

---

[128] Information Commissioner's Office (UK). (2021). *Opinion on the use of LFR in public places.*

[129] GDPR, Art. 22 – Automated individual decision-making and profiling

enforcement systems is generally classified as high-risk due to its potential impact on fundamental rights, privacy, and due process guarantees.[130]

In China, there is no unified, comprehensive framework for regulating artificial intelligence. Instead, the system operates on a sector-specific (sub-sectoral) principle, meaning that different rules apply to other technologies. In recent years, the government has focused on three key regulatory directions. The first was the 2022 Regulation on Algorithmic Recommendations, which governs how digital platforms design and use recommendation algorithms, emphasizing transparency, user awareness, and oversight of algorithmic operations.[131] In 2023, China introduced the Regulation on Deep Synthesis Technologies, commonly known as the deepfake regulation. This framework requires labeling content authenticity and imposes restrictions on false or manipulative content, aiming to prevent misinformation, deception, and reputational harm caused by AI-generated media.[132] In the same year, China's Regulation on Generative Artificial Intelligence came into force, focusing primarily on content moderation and the prevention of misinformation. This regulation seeks to ensure that AI-generated content aligns with public order, ethical standards, and state information policies, reinforcing government oversight over generative AI systems.[133] Starting in 2025, special regulations on facial recognition will also take effect in China. Under the new rules, the use of such technology in public spaces will be permitted only when strictly necessary for public safety purposes. Operators will be required to offer alternative authentication methods, ensure system transparency, and obtain prior consent from individuals whose biometric data is processed.

These regulations share a common foundation—a focus on informational control and security priorities. Platforms are obligated to manage their algorithms responsibly, implement effective content moderation, and combat misinformation. Meanwhile, facial recognition systems must operate solely within the framework of national security and always provide alternative means of identification to prevent overreliance

---

[130] European Commission. (2025). *AI Act Enforcement Guidelines.*

[131] Cyberspace Administration of China. (2022). *Provisions on the administration of algorithmic recommendations for internet information services.* http://www.cac.gov.cn/2022-01/04/c_1642894601871805.htm (Last access: 20.08.2025 წ.).

[132] Cyberspace Administration of China. (2023a). *Provisions on the administration of deep synthesis internet information services.* http://www.cac.gov.cn/2023-01/10/c_1674941327022722.htm (Last access: 17.08.2025 წ.).

[133] Cyberspace Administration of China. (2023b). *Interim measures for the management of generative artificial intelligence services.* http://www.cac.gov.cn/2023-07/13/c_1690898327022435.htm (Last access: 17.08.2025 წ.).

on biometric surveillance.[134] In China, artificial intelligence systems are already being used to process judicial decisions. In 2020, in one of the provinces, an AI system generated a preliminary judgment in a minor criminal case, which a human judge subsequently approved[135]. However, several critics have pointed out that such practices increase the risk of formalizing or diminishing the role of the judge, potentially undermining judicial discretion and the human element in the administration of justice.[136]

Estonia is widely regarded as one of the most successful examples of digital governance, built upon a network of interconnected technological systems. To advance the use of artificial intelligence in the public sector, Estonia launched a special national program called KrattAI. The goal of this initiative is to integrate AI into both public and private sector services, enabling citizens to interact with a unified digital environment. Under this concept, citizens can use a single "virtual assistant" to communicate with various government agencies, receive consultations, and handle documentation — with the system itself coordinating between different services. This model is often referred to as the "AI assistant for every citizen."[137] As mentioned above, Estonia also employs artificial intelligence to resolve minor disputes, and its experience is gradually expanding into criminal justice as well.[138] Despite its success, experts caution that applying such approaches in criminal law requires particular caution, given the sensitivity of individual rights and the high stakes involved in criminal proceedings.[139]

When examining international practice, it is particularly insightful to consider the approach of the European Court of Human Rights (ECHR) in such matters. As of today, the Court has not yet directly ruled on cases specifically concerning the use of artificial intelligence in criminal proceedings or investigations, but several judgments touch upon related issues.

One notable example is the case of *S. and Marper v. the United Kingdom*. On 4 December 2008, the ECHR delivered a landmark judgment concerning the protection of personal data, particularly biometric information. In this case, the UK police had

---

[134] Cyberspace Administration of China. (2025). *Provisions on the security management of facial recognition technology applications*. [coming into effect in 2025].

[135] Supreme People's Court of China. (2020). *Smart Court White Paper*.

[136] Zhang, W. (2021). *AI and Judicial Decision-Making in China. Tsinghua China Law Review*.

[137] e-Estonia. (2019). *KrattAI Strategy Factsheet*.

[138] Ministry of Justice of Estonia. (2021). *e-Justice Strategy 2021–2030*.

[139] Suksi, M. (2022). *Artificial Intelligence and Courts: Lessons from Estonia*.

retained the fingerprints and other biometric data of one juvenile and one adult for an indefinite period, even though both individuals had been cleared of criminal responsibility.[140] In fact, the police acted in accordance with existing national legal regulations, which at the time permitted the indefinite retention of such biometric data.[141] The applicants argued that this practice violated Article 8 of the European Convention on Human Rights, which guarantees the right to respect for private and family life. They contended that the presumption of innocence was undermined, and that the indefinite retention of their data created a risk of stigmatization, effectively portraying them as criminals despite their exoneration.[142] The United Kingdom government argued that data retention was an essential tool for crime investigation and prevention. Given its position, the DNA and fingerprint database frequently assisted in identifying suspects in both old and new cases, and storing such data did not constitute a disproportionate interference, as it was used solely for legitimate law enforcement purposes.[143] The Grand Chamber of the European Court of Human Rights ruled unanimously that the UK's practice violated Article 8 of the Convention. In its judgment, the Court emphasized that the indefinite retention of biometric data belonging to individuals who had never been convicted was disproportionate, especially in the absence of an adequate legal framework. The Court held that such a policy failed to strike a fair balance between the public interest and individual rights, resulting in an unjustified intrusion into private life and creating risks of discrimination and stigmatization.[144]

On 13 February 2020, the European Court of Human Rights delivered its judgment in *Gaughran v the United Kingdom*, a case concerning the retention of biometric data of convicted individuals and the right to privacy.

In this case, the applicant, Edward Gaughran, was arrested by police in Northern Ireland for driving under the influence of alcohol. A court later convicted him, fined, and temporarily disqualified from driving.[145] At the time of his arrest, the police collected his DNA sample, fingerprints, and photograph. Under the applicable

---

[140] European Court of Human Rights. (2008). *S. and Marper v. the United Kingdom* (Applications nos. 30562/04 and 30566/04), Applicants' submissions, § 54–57.

[141] Police and Criminal Evidence Act 1984, c. 60 (UK).

[142] European Court of Human Rights. (2008). *S. and Marper v. the United Kingdom* (Applications nos. 30562/04 and 30566/04), Applicants' submissions, § 54–57.

[143] Ibid., Government's submissions, § 68–73.

[144] European Court of Human Rights. (2008). *S. and Marper v. the United Kingdom* (Applications nos. 30562/04 and 30566/04), Judgment (Grand Chamber), § 125–126.

[145] *Gaughran v. the United Kingdom*, no. 45245/15, Judgment (ECHR, 13 February 2020), § 8–9

Northern Ireland legislation — the Police and Criminal Evidence (Northern Ireland) Order 1989 — these data could be retained indefinitely, regardless of the minor nature of the offence.[146] Gaughran applied to the Court, arguing that this practice violated Article 8 of the European Convention on Human Rights, which guarantees the right to respect for private and family life. He contended that the indefinite retention of his biometric data constituted a disproportionate interference, particularly given that the offence was relatively minor and that there was no mechanism for periodic review of the retention policy.[147] The government argued that retaining biometric data was an essential tool for crime prevention and investigation, noting that offender databases often played a crucial role in solving serious crimes. It maintained that indefinite retention was justified by public safety considerations, particularly given that the applicant had already been convicted, and therefore the practice was both reasonable and proportionate.[148] The Court unanimously found a violation of Article 8 of the Convention. In its judgment, the Court explained that although the applicant had been convicted, the indefinite retention of his biometric data was disproportionate, even in cases involving minor offences, where no clear time limits or mechanisms for periodic review existed. The Court emphasized that the protection of private life requires maintaining a fair balance between the rights of the individual and the interests of the state, and that the practice in question failed to uphold this balance, thereby constituting an unjustified interference with the applicant's right to privacy.[149]

On 17 October 2019, the Grand Chamber of the European Court of Human Rights delivered a significant judgment in the case of *López Ribalda and Others v. Spain*, concerning the legality of covert workplace video surveillance and the standards for protecting the right to private life.

In this case, the manager of a supermarket in Sant Celoni, Spain, noticed discrepancies between the warehouse stock levels and the cash register records. Suspecting theft, he installed two types of surveillance cameras:

---

[146] Police and Criminal Evidence (Northern Ireland) Order 1989, SI 1989/1341 (NI 12)

[147] *Gaughran v. the United Kingdom*, Applicants' submissions, § 54–58

[148] Ibid., Government's submissions, § 60–64

[149] *Gaughran v. the United Kingdom*, Judgment, § 85–88.

- Visible cameras, covering the store entrance, about which both employees and customers were informed, and
- Hidden cameras, aimed directly at the cash registers, of which the employees were not informed.[150]

The video recordings confirmed that several employees were stealing goods and, in some cases, giving them to others. Following this discovery, the employer dismissed all the implicated workers and filed a complaint with the police. The dismissed employees — including López Ribalda — brought a claim before the Spanish courts, arguing that the covert video surveillance violated their right to respect for private life under Article 8 of the European Convention on Human Rights.[151]

On 24 January 2019, the European Court of Human Rights delivered its judgment in the case of *Catt v. the United Kingdom*, which concerned the legality of police data collection and retention on individuals participating in demonstrations.

The applicant, John Catt, a British activist, had taken part in numerous peaceful protests, including demonstrations organized by the "Smash EDO" campaign — a movement opposing a British arms manufacturer. Catt was repeatedly recorded on police surveillance during these events, and his participation was entered into a police "Extremism Database," even though he had never engaged in any violent conduct nor had he ever been charged with an offence.

Catt filed a complaint in the UK courts, arguing that the collection and indefinite retention of information about him constituted a disproportionate interference with his private life, particularly considering his age and peaceful activism. He further argued that this practice posed a risk of political profiling, in violation of Article 8 of the European Convention on Human Rights.

The UK government contended that data retention served public safety and crime-prevention purposes, claiming it was necessary to monitor potential risks in activist environments. They emphasized that the data was used not to assess political opinions, but to maintain public order.

The Court found that the police's collection and retention of personal data did indeed constitute an interference with private life, and while such interference can

[150] *López Ribalda and Others v. Spain* [GC], nos. 1874/13 and 8567/13, Judgment (ECHR, 17 October 2019), § 10–15

[151] Ibid., Applicants' submissions, § 58–62.

sometimes be justified, the UK's system lacked sufficient safeguards to ensure that the data was not kept longer than necessary. The Court also underlined that the data contained details about the applicant's political views, an area subject to enhanced protection. Ultimately, the Court unanimously held that there had been a violation of Article 8, noting that Catt's data had been retained indefinitely, without clear rules governing its deletion or periodic review, and without precise criteria defining when continued retention was necessary.[152]

The European Court of Human Rights (ECtHR) has issued numerous other judgments concerning data retention and processing, which collectively demonstrate that the standards of Article 8 of the European Convention on Human Rights — the right to respect for private and family life — directly apply to modern technologies that may form the basis of artificial intelligence (AI) in criminal investigations.

As illustrated by the cases of *S. and Marper v. the United Kingdom* and *Gaughran v. the United Kingdom*, biometric data (such as DNA, fingerprints, and photographs) are highly sensitive, and their storage or processing within AI-driven systems requires clear retention periods, periodic review, and well-defined purposes. In the context of AI — where algorithms rely on large datasets — it is essential to ensure compliance with the principles of data minimization and purpose limitation throughout processing.

According to the ECtHR's interpretative approach, when AI systems are used in criminal investigations, the following safeguards must be taken into account:

- Proportionality test – An assessment must be made as to whether the data processing is necessary for a specific investigation and whether a less intrusive alternative could achieve the same purpose.
- Purpose limitation – Data and AI-driven analysis must be used solely for investigative purposes, without extending to unrelated contexts.
- Retention periods and review mechanisms – Data collected for investigative purposes must be deleted or anonymized after a reasonable period when no longer needed.
- Independent oversight – The processing of data by AI systems must be subject to judicial or independent supervisory control, ensuring legality and accountability.

[152] *Catt v. the United Kingdom*, no. 43514/15, Judgment (ECHR, 24 January 2019), § 8–14.

- Protection of special categories of data – Information concerning political opinions, health, biometric identifiers, or journalistic sources requires enhanced safeguards, even when used for crime prevention purposes.
- Algorithmic transparency and auditability – There must be a mechanism to verify and audit how the algorithm functions, to prevent discrimination or arbitrariness.

These principles, derived from European human rights jurisprudence, provide a foundation for regulating the use of AI in criminal justice systems, balancing technological innovation with the protection of individual rights.

Table N1

Country	AI Legal Framework	Data Protection Approach
United States	No strictly uniform approach. The 2023 Presidential Executive Order focuses on the safety and trustworthiness of AI. Some states (e.g., California) have adopted their own AI regulations. The main emphasis is on constitutional rights (due process and equal protection).	Decentralized; general federal standards exist, but state-level rules vary.
European Union	EU AI Act + GDPR; strict regulations on high-risk AI systems, requiring transparency and human oversight.	GDPR – strict standards emphasizing data minimization and purpose limitation.
China	State-driven and centralized regulation; broad use of AI in the judicial system, with limited transparency.	State-controlled data; personal data protection is less stringent.
Estonia	Focus on e-Justice platforms and digital public services; use of AI for small claims in accordance with legal and ethical principles.	Strict data protection similar to the GDPR; state IT infrastructure built with high security standards.

5.2. Successful Cases and Failures

Estonia has implemented a unified digital service network in the public sector, integrating hundreds of small-scale AI applications — such as automated document processing and AI-generated responses to citizen inquiries, particularly in areas like taxation and social services.[153] The system operates on an open architecture and is built around a strict principle of human oversight, which excludes fully automated decision-making in judicial or law enforcement contexts.[154]

Within the European Union, under the STAR Project, law enforcement agencies have implemented high-risk AI tools — such as biometric data comparison systems — only with strict prior authorization and real-time human oversight.[155] This approach has significantly reduced false positive results and helped prevent legal disputes related to human rights violations.[156]

In 2023, the Los Angeles Police Department (LAPD) implemented a locally developed AI-based resource allocation system that relied solely on geographical indicators, rather than individual profiling.[157] As a result, the initiative led to a significant improvement in crime prevention rates.[158]

Despite the positive experiences mentioned above, several AI systems have failed in practice. One such example is the "SyRI" (System Risk Indication) program implemented in the Netherlands. In 2020, the court declared the system unlawful, ruling that it relied on an opaque algorithm and lacked sufficient legal grounds for the mass processing of personal data.[159] The court found that the system violated Article 8 of the European Convention on Human Rights (the right to respect for private life) and was disproportionate in relation to its intended purpose.[160]

The COMPAS program, used in criminal proceedings, was found to exhibit racial bias, as confirmed by a 2016 investigation by ProPublica.[161] The study found that Black defendants were twice as likely to be classified by the system as "high risk," despite having lower actual rates of reoffending. This case sparked a long-standing national debate in the United States about algorithmic fairness, racial bias, and transparency in AI-driven justice systems.[162]

---

[153] e-Estonia. (2024). *AI in Public Sector is a Team Sport.*

[154] Ministry of Justice of Estonia. (2022). *Official clarification: Estonia does not develop an AI judge.*

[155] European Commission. (2023). *STAR Project Overview.*

[156] Europol. (2024). *Fundamental Rights Impact Assessments in AI Deployment.*

[157] Los Angeles Police Department. (2023). *Predictive Policing Pilot – Resource Allocation Model.*

[158] Brennan Center for Justice. (2024). *AI and Constitutional Policing.*

[159] Hague District Court. (2020). *ECLI:NL:RBDHA:2020:1878 (SyRI).*

[160] Privacy International. (2020). *Dutch Court Ruling on SyRI.*

[161] ProPublica. (2016). *Machine Bias.*

[162] Harvard Law Review. (2019). *Disparate Impact in Algorithmic Risk Assessment.*

In several Chinese cities, the mass facial recognition systems implemented by authorities were criticized by Amnesty International, as they were allegedly used to identify participants in demonstrations and monitor political activists.[163] This practice failed to meet the principles of purpose limitation and was linked to the persecution of human rights defenders.[164]

5.3. Issues Related to Appealing Decisions Made by Artificial Intelligence

The protection of personal data is a fundamental aspect of AI regulation. The European standard on personal data protection (GDPR) establishes the core principles of data processing — lawfulness, transparency, purpose limitation, data minimization, accuracy, and security.[165] In the law enforcement sector, where sensitive categories of data — including biometric information — are frequently processed, additional restrictions apply under the aforementioned standard.[166]

At the international level, both the OECD Privacy Guidelines and the Council of Europe Convention 108 — *the Convention for the Protection of Individuals with regard to Automatic Processing of Personal Data* — oblige states and the private sector to ensure data protection throughout the entire lifecycle of artificial intelligence systems.[167] In high-risk AI projects, it is particularly essential to establish a comprehensive risk assessment framework and apply it proactively to prevent privacy violations and ensure compliance with human rights and data protection standards.[168]

Human oversight of the operation of artificial intelligence systems ensures that decisions made by such systems are not executed automatically and remain subject to human intervention at all times. The EU Artificial Intelligence Act stipulates that high-risk AI systems must be designed so that a human operator can interrupt, modify, or review the system's functioning and the outcomes it produces.[169]

---

[163] Amnesty International. (2021). *China: Mass Surveillance and Human Rights.*

[164] Human Rights Watch. (2022). *China's Algorithms of Repression.*

[165] Regulation (EU) 2016/679 (GDPR), Art. 5 – Principles relating to processing of personal data.

[166] Regulation (EU) 2016/679 (GDPR), Art. 9 – Processing of special categories of personal data.

[167] OECD. (2013). *OECD Guidelines on the Protection of Privacy and Transborder Flows of Personal Data.*

[168] Regulation (EU) 2016/679 (GDPR), Art. 35 – Data Protection Impact Assessment.

[169] Regulation (EU) 2024/1689 (AI Act), Art. 14 – Human oversight requirements.

The OECD Privacy Guidelines also emphasize that the responsible use of artificial intelligence systems requires human oversight at both the technical and legal levels.[170] This entails establishing mechanisms that enable effective system control and auditability, ensuring that human supervisors can verify the source and rationale of AI-generated decisions.[171]

Algorithmic transparency means that the operation of an AI system and its decision-making process must be explainable and understandable not only to developers, but also to users and regulators. The General Data Protection Regulation (GDPR) obliges organizations to ensure that individuals subject to automated decisions have the "right to an explanation" — that is, the right to understand why a specific decision was made about them.[172] The "black box" effect must be avoided in the use of artificial intelligence, ensuring that the system's internal logic and decision-making processes remain transparent and interpretable.[173] In practice, this involves implementing technical methods such as recording intermediate model states, maintaining detailed logs, and documenting the algorithm's behavior to ensure traceability and accountability throughout the system's operation.[174]

---

[170] OECD. (2019). *OECD Principles on Artificial Intelligence.*

[171] Floridi, L., & Cowls, J. (2019). *A Unified Framework of Five Principles for AI in Society. Harvard Data Science Review*, 1(1).

[172] Regulation (EU) 2016/679 (GDPR), Art. 22 – Automated individual decision-making, including profiling.

[173] High-Level Expert Group on AI. (2019). *Ethics Guidelines for Trustworthy AI.* European Commission.

[174] Doshi-Velez, F., & Kim, B. (2017). *Towards a Rigorous Science of Interpretable Machine Learning*. arXiv:1702.08608.

Chapter VI. Conclusions and Recommendations

6.1. The Potential of Technology in Criminal Law

Artificial intelligence has the potential to significantly enhance investigative processes — from large-scale data analysis to the automated processing of digital evidence.[175] Such systems facilitate the rapid identification of video and audio materials, transcription of recordings, classification of textual data, and detection of anomalies.[176] These technologies are particularly effective in cases involving cybercrime, financial fraud, and organized crime.[177]

Artificial intelligence can analyze and predict trends in criminal behavior, enabling law enforcement agencies to implement targeted preventive measures.[178] For example, predictive policing systems use historical statistical data to identify areas or time periods with a high crime risk.[179] However, such systems must be designed to prevent discriminatory profiling and ensure compliance with equality standards.[180]

In judicial proceedings, artificial intelligence can assist judges and prosecutors in processing large volumes of legal documents, identifying precedents, and comparing evidence.[181] AI-assisted legal research reduces time and resource expenditures while enhancing the consistency of decisions and conclusions.[182]

Through artificial intelligence, it is possible to verify the authenticity of digital evidence — for instance, by analyzing deepfakes and examining the metadata of media

[175] McCue, C. (2022). *Data Mining and Predictive Analysis: Intelligence Gathering and Crime Analysis*. Elsevier.
[176] Jain, A., & Singh, A. (2021). *AI Applications in Digital Forensics. Forensic Science International: Digital Investigation*, 38, 301207.
[177] Europol. (2022). *Internet Organised Crime Threat Assessment (IOCTA)*.
[178] Perry, W. L., et al. (2013). *Predictive Policing: The Role of Crime Forecasting in Law Enforcement Operations*. RAND Corporation.
[179] Ferguson, A. G. (2017). *The Rise of Big Data Policing: Surveillance, Race, and the Future of Law Enforcement*. NYU Press.
[180] Lum, K., & Isaac, W. (2016). *To predict and serve?. Significance*, 13(5), 14–19.
[181] Aletras, N., Tsarapatsanis, D., Preoţiuc-Pietro, D., & Lampos, V. (2016). *Predicting judicial decisions of the European Court of Human Rights. PeerJ Computer Science*, 2, e93.
[182] Ashley, K. D. (2017). *Artificial Intelligence and Legal Analytics*. Cambridge University Press.

files.[183] This is critically important in modern digital-age courts, where falsifying visual or audio evidence has become increasingly easy.[184]

The implementation of artificial intelligence within law enforcement agencies reduces operational costs and increases efficiency by enabling better allocation of human resources.[185]

6.2. Main Risks and Their Prevention

One of the main risks in artificial intelligence systems is algorithmic bias, which may arise from historically biased data or flawed model architecture.[186] This issue is particularly critical in criminal law, where biased predictions can lead to unfair arrests or pretrial detentions.[187] A notable example is the COMPAS system used in the United States, which, according to a ProPublica investigation, often rated Black defendants as higher-risk individuals compared to white defendants.[188]

Obviously, these risks do not mean that artificial intelligence should not be used in this field. In such cases, what is needed is the prudent prevention of risks, including:

- The use of diverse and balanced datasets;[189]
- Regular monitoring by independent bodies to eliminate algorithmic bias;[190]
- Ensuring that the algorithm is transparent and explainable.[191]

---

[183] Verdoliva, L. (2020). *Media Forensics and Deepfakes: An Overview. IEEE Journal of Selected Topics in Signal Processing*, 14(5), 910–932.

[184] Agarwal, S., Farid, H., Gu, Y., He, M., Nagano, K., & Li, H. (2019). *Protecting World Leaders Against Deep Fakes. CVPR Workshops.*

[185] Deloitte. (2020). *AI in the Public Sector: Opportunities and Challenges.*

[186] Barocas, S., Hardt, M., & Narayanan, A. (2023). *Fairness and Machine Learning.*

[187] Angwin, J., Larson, J., Mattu, S., & Kirchner, L. (2016). *Machine Bias*. ProPublica.

[188] Ibid.

[189] Mehrabi, N., et al. (2021). *A Survey on Bias and Fairness in Machine Learning. ACM Computing Surveys*, 54(6).

[190] Raji, I. D., & Buolamwini, J. (2019). *Actionable Auditing. AAAI/ACM Conference on AI, Ethics, and Society.*

[191] Doshi-Velez, F., & Kim, B. (2017). *Towards a Rigorous Science of Interpretable Machine Learning.*

In law enforcement systems, artificial intelligence often relies on personal and biometric data, creating serious privacy risks.[192] For example, mass facial recognition programs in China and certain other jurisdictions have led to human rights violations and the identification of political activists.[193] Accordingly, in such cases, effective risk prevention requires:

- The implementation of strict data protection frameworks (e.g., GDPR, Convention 108+);[194]
- Risk assessment for high-risk projects;[195]
- Adherence to the principle of processing only the minimum necessary data (data minimization).[196]

Many artificial intelligence systems are difficult to explain, creating a "black box" effect that limits the ability to verify the decision-making process.[197] In criminal law, this risk may manifest when a defendant cannot obtain an explanation of the reasoning behind a decision.[198] Accordingly, to counter this risk, it is essential to:

- Use understandable and explainable technologies;[199]
- Maintain logs of algorithmic decisions;[200]
- Ensure open documentation of models and independent expert review.[201]

New technologies, such as Deepfake, create the risk that evidence presented in court may be falsified.[202] This danger is amplified by the spread of social media and open sources, where verifying authenticity is difficult.[203] Therefore, in this case, it is necessary to:

---

[192] GDPR, Art. 5 & Art. 9 – Data protection principles and sensitive data.
[193] Human Rights Watch. (2022). *China's Algorithms of Repression.*
[194] OECD. (2013). *OECD Guidelines on the Protection of Privacy*
[195] GDPR, Art. 35 – Data Protection Impact Assessment.
[196] Regulation (EU) 2016/679 (GDPR), Art. 5(1)(c) – Data minimization principle
[197] Burrell, J. (2016). *How the machine 'thinks'. Big Data & Society*, 3(1).
[198] GDPR, Art. 22 – Automated decision-making, including profiling.
[199] Gunning, D., & Aha, D. W. (2019). *DARPA's Explainable AI Program. AI Magazine*, 40(2).
[200] Floridi, L., & Cowls, J. (2019). *A Unified Framework of Five Principles for AI in Societ*
[201] High-Level Expert Group on AI. (2019). *Ethics Guidelines for Trustworthy AI.*
[202] Verdoliva, L. (2020). *Media Forensics and Deepfakes: An Overview. IEEE Journal of Selected Topics in Signal Processing*, 14(5).
[203] Agarwal, S., et al. (2019). *Protecting World Leaders Against Deep Fakes. CVPR Workshops.*

- Implement technologies for verifying the authenticity of media files;[204]
- Train specialized experts to examine digital evidence;[205]
- Ensure strict control over the digital evidence chain of custody.[206]

The widespread automated use of artificial intelligence systems may lead to situations where the system makes final decisions without human intervention.[207] This undermines fundamental legal principles such as the right to a fair trial and carries multiple associated risks.[208] Therefore, in this context, it is of fundamental importance to:

- Strengthen the legal obligation for human oversight;[209]
- Design systems with a "stop button" and the possibility of human review;[210]
- Ensure independent verification of decisions.[211]

6.3. Recommendations for Policy and Practice

States should develop national strategies for the use of artificial intelligence that include specific provisions for its application in law enforcement and criminal justice.[212] This document should reflect the ethical principles governing AI use, data protection standards, transparency obligations, and guarantees of human oversight over AI decision-making.[213]

It is advisable to establish relevant ethics councils composed of lawyers, technologists, IT specialists, and representatives of civil society.[214] The function of such councils would be to evaluate artificial intelligence systems before their implementation and to conduct their periodic monitoring.[215]

---

[204] Ibid.
[205] Jain, A., & Singh, A. (2021). *AI Applications in Digital Forensics*.
[206] Casey, E., et al. (2019). *Digital Evidence and Computer Crime*. Academic Press.
[207] AI Act, Art. 14 – Human oversight requirements.
[208] Ferguson, A. G. (2017). *The Rise of Big Data Policing*.
[209] OECD. (2019). *OECD Principles on Artificial Intelligence*.
[210] AI Act, Annex III – Technical requirements for high-risk AI systems.
[211] European Commission. (2025). *AI Act Enforcement Guidelines*.
[212] OECD. (2019). *OECD Principles on Artificial Intelligence*
[213] High-Level Expert Group on AI. (2019). *Ethics Guidelines for Trustworthy AI*.
[214] Floridi, L., & Cowls, J. (2019). *A Unified Framework of Five Principles for AI in Society*
[215] Raji, I. D., & Buolamwini, J. (2019). *Actionable Auditing. AIES Conference.*

When implementing such systems, it is essential to establish a unified registry that includes all active systems, their purposes, their scope of use, and the risk assessments conducted.[216] This will ensure public trust and uphold individuals' right to know how and for what purposes the technology is being used.[217]

National legislation should take into account the requirements set forth in the international instruments discussed above.[218] This will ensure that domestic regulations align with internationally recognized best practices, ultimately contributing to a unified and secure global environment.[219]

For high-risk artificial intelligence systems, the law should mandate compulsory human oversight — meaning that any decision made by an AI system cannot become final without human intervention.[220]

Legislation should ensure the transparency and explainability of algorithms, including the provision of source code or technical documentation to relevant authorities.[221] Additionally, it should mandate logging of algorithmic decisions.[222] Periodic independent audits of artificial intelligence systems are essential to verify both technical and legal compliance.[223] The results of such audits should be made public, except in cases involving national security considerations.[224]

It is advisable to integrate a so-called "stop button" and review mechanisms into all high-risk systems.[225] Additionally, data anonymization and pseudonymization should be implemented wherever possible.[226]

Active participation in international forums and platforms dedicated to developing legal and technical standards for artificial intelligence is recommended.[227]

---

[216] European Commission. (2023). *AI Transparency Requirements under the AI Act.*

[217] AI Now Institute. (2018). *Algorithmic Accountability Policy Toolkit.*

[218] Regulation (EU) 2024/1689 (AI Act).

[219] GDPR, Regulation (EU) 2016/679.

[220] AI Act, Art. 14 – Human oversight.

[221] Doshi-Velez, F., & Kim, B. (2017). *Towards a Rigorous Science of Interpretable Machine Learning.*

[222] AI Act, Annex III – Technical documentation requirements.

[223] Kroll, J. A., et al. (2017). *Accountable Algorithms. University of Pennsylvania Law Review,* 165(3).

[224] Privacy International. (2020). *Algorithmic Impact Assessments.*

[225] AI Act, Art. 14 & Annex III.

[226] GDPR, Art. 25 – Data protection by design and by default.

[227] UNICRI & INTERPOL. (2021). *AI for Law Enforcement: Opportunities and Challenges.*

Such engagement will facilitate the exchange of experience and the adaptation of best practices to the local context.[228]

6.4. Future Scenario

In the next 10–15 years, it is expected that artificial intelligence systems will be capable of performing nearly fully automated analyses of evidence — including the processing of video footage, audio recordings, phone logs, and social media data — with minimal human intervention.[229] While this will accelerate the pace of investigations, it will also intensify challenges related to transparency.[230]

Artificial intelligence may become integrated into tactical decision-making processes — for instance, providing patrol units with real-time data analysis and recommendations for optimal actions.[231] While this will enhance operational efficiency, it will also require a clear legal framework to prevent discriminatory profiling.[232]

The development of quantum computing could radically change the capabilities of artificial intelligence, particularly in processing large volumes of data and breaking encryption systems.[233] This may positively affect criminal investigations, but it could also lead to new forms of cybercrime.[234]

Two possible scenarios may unfold:

a. International standard harmonization, in which countries develop unified regulations governing the use of artificial intelligence in investigation and criminal proceedings; or

---

[228] Council of Europe. (2022). *Guidelines on Artificial Intelligence and Data Protection.*

[229] Jain, A., & Singh, A. (2021). *AI Applications in Digital Forensics. Forensic Science International: Digital Investigation*, 38, 301207.

[230] Ferguson, A. G. (2017). *The Rise of Big Data Policing.* NYU Press.

[231] UNICRI & INTERPOL. (2021). *AI for Law Enforcement: Opportunities and Challenges.*

[232] Lum, K., & Isaac, W. (2016). *To predict and serve?. Significance*, 13(5), 14–19.

[233] Gyongyosi, L., & Imre, S. (2019). *A Survey on Quantum Computing Technology. Computer Science Review*, 31, 51–71.

[234] Mosca, M. (2018). *Cybersecurity in an Era with Quantum Computers. IEEE Security & Privacy*, 16(5), 38–41.

b. Legal fragmentation, where different jurisdictions establish incompatible frameworks. [235]The first scenario would promote international cooperation, while the second would complicate evidence exchange and joint investigations.[236]

Moreover, artificial intelligence systems could become officially recognized as "virtual experts," whose conclusions would carry evidentiary status in court proceedings.[237] This, however, would raise critical questions regarding accountability, transparency, and the protection of defendants' rights.[238]

---

[235] Regulation (EU) 2024/1689 (AI Act).

[236] Council of Europe. (2022). *Guidelines on Artificial Intelligence and Data Protection.*

[237] Ashley, K. D. (2017). *Artificial Intelligence and Legal Analytics*. Cambridge University Press.

[238] Burrell, J. (2016). *How the machine 'thinks'. Big Data & Society*, 3(1).

Bibliography

Legal Instruments and Normative Sources:

1. Amnesty International. (2021). *China: Mass surveillance and human rights.* Amnesty International Report.
2. Brennan Center for Justice. (2024). *AI and constitutional policing.* Brennan Center for Justice.
3. Bundesverfassungsgericht. (2023). *Press release on the Hesse/Hamburg automated police data analysis ruling.* Federal Constitutional Court of Germany.
4. European Court of Human Rights. (2023). *Guide on Article 6 of the European Convention on Human Rights.* Strasbourg: Registry of the Court.
5. European Commission. (2023). *Algorithms, rule of law, and the future of justice.* Luxembourg: Publications Office of the European Union.
6. European Commission. (2023). *STAR project overview.* Brussels: European Commission.
7. Europol. (2022). *Internet organised crime threat assessment (IOCTA).* The Hague: Europol.
8. Europol. (2024). *Fundamental rights impact assessments in AI deployment.* The Hague: Europol.
9. High-Level Expert Group on AI. (2019). *Ethics guidelines for trustworthy AI.* European Commission.
10. Human Rights Watch. (2022). *China's algorithms of repression.* Human Rights Watch Report.
11. Information Commissioner's Office (UK). (2021). *Opinion on the use of live facial recognition (LFR) in public places.* London: ICO.
12. Ministry of Justice of Estonia. (2021). *e-Justice Strategy 2021–2030.* Tallinn: Ministry of Justice.
13. Ministry of Justice of Estonia. (2022). *Official clarification: Estonia does not develop an AI judge.* Tallinn: Ministry of Justice.
14. Supreme People's Court of China. (2020). *Smart court white paper.* Beijing: SPC Press.
15. Supreme People's Court of China. (2023). *Annual report on the application of artificial intelligence in courts.* Beijing: SPC Press.
16. UNICRI & INTERPOL. (2021). *AI for law enforcement: Opportunities and challenges.* United Nations Interregional Crime and Justice Research Institute.

Judicial Decisions:

1. Bundesverfassungsgericht. (2023). *Press release on the Hesse/Hamburg automated police data analysis ruling.* Federal Constitutional Court of Germany.
2. European Court of Human Rights. (2021). *Big Brother Watch and Others v. the United Kingdom,* Apps. Nos. 58170/13, 62322/14, and 24960/15 (Grand Chamber judgment, 25 May 2021).
3. European Court of Human Rights. (2023). *Guide on Article 6 of the European Convention on Human Rights.* Strasbourg: Registry of the Court.
4. State v. Loomis, 881 N.W.2d 749 (Wis. 2016).
5. The Hague District Court (Netherlands). (2020). *NJCM c.s./Netherlands (SyRI judgment).*

Scientific Monographs, Articles, and Reports

1. Aletras, N., Tsarapatsanis, D., Preoţiuc-Pietro, D., & Lampos, V. (2016). Predicting judicial decisions of the European Court of Human Rights. *PeerJ Computer Science, 2.*
2. Aleven, V., & Ashley, K. D. (1997). Teaching case-based argumentation through interactive multimedia. *Artificial Intelligence and Law, 5*(2–4), 193–218.
3. Amnesty International. (2021). *China: Mass surveillance and human rights.*
4. Angwin, J., Larson, J., Mattu, S., & Kirchner, L. (2016). Machine bias. *ProPublica.*
5. Apollonius Rhodius. (2007). *Argonautica* (R. Hunter, Trans.). Oxford University Press. (Original work published ca. 3rd century BCE).
6. Ashley, K. D. (1990). *Modeling legal argument: Reasoning with cases and hypotheticals.* MIT Press.
7. Barocas, S., Hardt, M., & Narayanan, A. (2023). *Fairness and machine learning.* MIT Press.
8. Bench-Capon, T., & Atkinson, K. (2021). Argumentation in artificial intelligence and law. *Artificial Intelligence.*
9. Berk, R. (2019). Accuracy and fairness for juvenile justice risk assessments. *Journal of Empirical Legal Studies, 16*(1).
10. Billah, M. (2025). Developing an explainable AI system for digital forensics: Enhancing trust and transparency in flagging events for legal evidence. *Journal of Forensic Science Research, 9*(2), 109–116.

11. Bostrom, N. (2014). *Superintelligence: Paths, dangers, strategies.* Oxford University Press.
12. Brantingham, J. P., Valasik, M., & Mohler, G. O. (2018). Does predictive policing lead to biased arrests? *Statistics and Public Policy, 5*(1).
13. Bratton, W. J., & Malinowski, S. W. (2008). Police performance management in practice: Taking COMPSTAT to the next level. *Policing: A Journal of Policy and Practice, 2*(3), 259–265.
14. Brennan Center for Justice. (2024). *AI and constitutional policing.*
15. Breuker, J., et al. (2009). The ESTRELLA project: Standardizing legal knowledge. *Knowledge Engineering Review, 24*(3), 251–275.
16. Brueckner, J., et al. (2009). [merged into Breuker ref → already included].
17. Buchanan, B. G., & Feigenbaum, E. A. (1978). DENDRAL and Meta-DENDRAL: Their applications dimension. *Artificial Intelligence, 11*(1–2), 5–24.
18. Buolamwini, J., & Gebru, T. (2018). Gender shades: Intersectional accuracy disparities in commercial gender classification. In *Proceedings of the 1st Conference on Fairness, Accountability and Transparency* (pp. 77–91).
19. Burrell, J. (2016). How the machine 'thinks': Understanding opacity in machine learning algorithms. *Big Data & Society, 3*(1).
20. Byrnes, M. (2021). Artificial intelligence and procedural fairness in courts. *Judicial Review, 26*(3).
21. Casey, E., Ferraro, M., & Nguyen, L. (2022). Digital evidence in the courtroom: AI-based assessment and admissibility. *Digital Investigation.*
22. Crevier, D. (1993). *AI: The tumultuous history of the search for artificial intelligence.* Basic Books.
23. Deloitte. (2020). *AI in the public sector: Opportunities and challenges.*
24. Doshi-Velez, F., & Kim, B. (2017). Towards a rigorous science of interpretable machine learning. *arXiv:1702.08608.*
25. Tribe, L. H. (2000). *American constitutional law* (3rd ed.). Foundation Press.
26. European Commission. (2021). *Proposal for a regulation laying down harmonised rules on artificial intelligence (Artificial Intelligence Act).*
27. European Commission. (2023). *Algorithms, rule of law, and the future of justice.*
28. European Commission. (2023). *STAR project overview.*
29. European Court of Human Rights. (2023). *Guide on Article 6 of the European Convention on Human Rights.*
30. European Law Blog. (2024). Predictive policing in the AI Act: Meaningful ban or paper tiger?

31. European Union. (2023). *Algorithms, rule of law, and the future of justice.*
32. Europol. (2022). *Internet organised crime threat assessment (IOCTA).*
33. Europol. (2024). *Fundamental rights impact assessments in AI deployment.*
34. Fenton, N., & Neil, M. (2019). *Risk assessment and decision analysis with Bayesian networks.* CRC Press.
35. Ferguson, A. G. (2017). *The rise of big data policing.* NYU Press.
36. Feldstein, S. (2019). *The global expansion of AI surveillance.* Carnegie Endowment for International Peace.
37. Fitzgerald, J., & Winters, C. (2021). Natural language processing in criminal profiling: Opportunities and risks. *Journal of Investigative Psychology and Offender Profiling, 18*(3).
38. Floridi, L., & Cowls, J. (2019). A unified framework of five principles for AI in society. *Harvard Data Science Review, 1*(1).
39. Garvie, C., Bedoya, A., & Frankle, J. (2016). *The perpetual lineup: Unregulated police face recognition in America.* Georgetown Law Center on Privacy & Technology.
40. Gunning, D., & Aha, D. W. (2019). DARPA's explainable AI program. *AI Magazine, 40*(2).
41. Gyongyosi, L., & Imre, S. (2019). A survey on quantum computing technology. *Computer Science Review, 31.*
42. Harvard Law Review. (2019). Disparate impact in algorithmic risk assessment.
43. Hassani, H., Huang, X., & Silva, E. (2020). Digitalisation and big data in criminal justice. *Applied Economics, 52*(14).
44. Henderson, P. (2022). Machine learning applications in behavioral crime analysis: The UK experience. *Policing: A Journal of Policy and Practice, 16*(4).
45. Hert, P., & Papakonstantinou, V. (2021). The GDPR and artificial intelligence: Law and ethics in the digital age. *Computer Law & Security Review, 41.*
46. High-Level Expert Group on AI. (2019). *Ethics guidelines for trustworthy AI.* European Commission.
47. Howard, P., & Dixon, L. (2019). The construction and validation of OASys. *Criminal Behaviour and Mental Health, 29*(1).
48. Human Rights Watch. (2022). *China's algorithms of repression.*
49. Information Commissioner's Office (UK). (2021). *Opinion on the use of LFR in public places.*
50. Jain, A., & Singh, A. (2021). AI applications in digital forensics. *Forensic Science International: Digital Investigation, 38,* 301207.
51. Johnson, L., & Patel, R. (2024). Machine learning in large-scale financial crime investigations. *International Journal of Digital Evidence.*

52. Johnson, R., & Miller, T. (2023). OSINT and big data analytics in urban policing. *Journal of Law Enforcement Technology, 8*(2).
53. Kroll, J. A., et al. (2017). Accountable algorithms. *University of Pennsylvania Law Review, 165*(3).
54. Krizhevsky, A., Sutskever, I., & Hinton, G. E. (2012). ImageNet classification with deep convolutional neural networks. *Communications of the ACM, 60*(6), 84–90.
55. Kõiv, M., & Laanemets, J. (2023). AI-driven OSINT in cybercrime investigations: The Estonian experience. *Baltic Journal of Law & Technology, 12*(3).
56. LandMark judgment from the Netherlands on digital welfare states and human rights. (2024). *Open Global Rights.*
57. Larson, J., Mattu, S., Kirchner, L., & Angwin, J. (2016). How we analyzed the COMPAS recidivism algorithm. *ProPublica.*
58. LeCun, Y., Bengio, Y., & Hinton, G. (2015). Deep learning. *Nature, 521*(7553), 436–444.
59. Lighthill, J. (1973). Artificial intelligence: A general survey. In *Artificial Intelligence: A paper symposium* (pp. 1–20). Science Research Council, UK.
60. Liu, H. (2020). Smart courts in China: Opportunities and challenges. *Computer Law & Security Review, 36.*
61. Los Angeles Police Department. (2023). *Predictive policing pilot – Resource allocation model.*
62. Luo, J., Zhang, Y., & Li, M. (2022). Smart courts and judicial efficiency in China: Empirical evidence and future prospects. *International Journal of Law and Information Technology, 30*(3).
63. Lum, K., & Isaac, W. (2016). To predict and serve? *Significance, 13*(5), 14–19.
64. Lum, K., & Isaac, W. (2021). To predict and serve? Predictive policing and civil rights. *Annual Review of Law and Social Science, 17.*
65. Mak, V. (2021). The impact of artificial intelligence on judicial decision-making in civil law. *Netherlands Journal of Legal Philosophy, 50*(1).
66. Matsumoto, R. (2024). AI-driven criminal profiling in homicide investigations: A Japanese perspective. *Asian Journal of Criminology, 19*(1).
67. Mayor, A. (2018). *Gods and robots: Myths, machines, and ancient dreams of technology.* Princeton University Press.
68. McCarthy, J. (2007). What is artificial intelligence? [Online manuscript].
69. McCarthy, J., Minsky, M. L., Rochester, N., & Shannon, C. E. (1955). A proposal for the Dartmouth summer research project on artificial intelligence.

70. McCarty, L. T. (1977). Reflections on "Taxman": An experiment in artificial intelligence and legal reasoning. *Harvard Law Review, 90*(5), 837–893.
71. McCue, C. (2022). *Data mining and predictive analysis: Intelligence gathering and crime analysis.* Elsevier.
72. McMillan, J. (2022). Artificial intelligence in court case management: Efficiency and fairness. *Journal of Law and Technology, 18*(2).
73. Mehrabi, N., et al. (2021). A survey on bias and fairness in machine learning. *ACM Computing Surveys, 54*(6).
74. Mohler, G. O., Short, M. B., Brantingham, P. J., Schoenberg, F. P., & Tita, G. E. (2015). Randomized controlled field trials of predictive policing. *Journal of the American Statistical Association, 110*(512), 1399–1411.
75. Mosca, M. (2018). Cybersecurity in an era with quantum computers. *IEEE Security & Privacy, 16*(5).
76. Moynihan, C. (2020, February 10). Dutch court blocks use of algorithmic risk scoring system for welfare fraud detection. *Just Security.*
77. Murray, A. T. (Trans.). (1919). *Apollonius Rhodius: Argonautica.* Loeb Classical Library. Harvard University Press.
78. Ng, M. (2021). Digital transformation in Singapore's judiciary: The eLitigation experience. *Asian Journal of Law and Society.*
79. Newell, A., & Simon, H. A. (1956). The logic theory machine—a complex information processing system. *IRE Transactions on Information Theory, 2*(3), 61–79.
80. Newell, A., Shaw, J. C., & Simon, H. A. (1959). Report on a general problem-solving program. In *Proceedings of the International Conference on Information Processing* (pp. 256–264). UNESCO.
81. Nilsson, N. J. (1998). *Artificial intelligence: A new synthesis.* Morgan Kaufmann.
82. O'Donnell, R. M. (2019). Challenging racist predictive policing algorithms under the Equal Protection Clause. *New York University Law Review.*
83. Oswald, M. (2021). Algorithmic risk assessment and the right to a fair trial. *Criminal Law Review, 6.*
84. Pauwels, L., Kindt, E., & Ponsaers, P. (2022). Ethical challenges in big data policing: Transparency and accountability. *Policing and Society, 32*(5).
85. Perry, W. L., et al. (2013). *Predictive policing: The role of crime forecasting in law enforcement operations.* RAND Corporation.
86. Privacy International. (2020). *Algorithmic impact assessments.*
87. Privacy International. (2020). Dutch court ruling on SyRI.
88. ProPublica. (2016). Machine bias.

89. Raji, I. D., & Buolamwini, J. (2019). Actionable auditing. In *AAAI/ACM Conference on AI, Ethics, and Society.*
90. Richardson, R., Schultz, J. M., & Crawford, K. (2019). Dirty data, bad predictions: How civil rights violations impact police data, predictive policing systems, and justice. *New York University Law Review Online.*
91. Ridley, M., Young, M., & Taylor, R. (2022). Publicly available information in criminal investigations: OSINT perspectives. *Police Practice and Research, 23*(4).
92. Raji, I. D., & Buolamwini, J. (2019). Actionable auditing. *AIES Conference.* [duplicate merged above].
93. Richardson, R., Schultz, J., & Crawford, K. (2019). [duplicate merged into NYU Law Review Online ref above].
94. Rudin, C., Wang, C., & Coker, B. (2020). The age of secrecy and unfairness in recidivism prediction. *Harvard Data Science Review, 2*(1).
95. Russell, S. J., & Norvig, P. (2021). *Artificial intelligence: A modern approach* (4th ed.). Pearson.
96. Salfati, C. G., Horning, A., & Sorochinski, M. (2022). Behavioral crime linkage and offender profiling: Integrating AI technologies. *Police Practice and Research, 23*(5).
97. Saunders, J., Hunt, P., & Hollywood, J. S. (2016). Predictions put into practice: A quasi-experimental evaluation of Chicago's predictive policing pilot. *Journal of Experimental Criminology, 12*(3), 347–371.
98. State v. Loomis, 881 N.W.2d 749 (Wis. 2016).
99. Stevenson, M. T., & Doleac, J. L. (2021). Algorithmic risk assessment in the hands of humans. *The Journal of Law, Economics, & Organization, 37*(3).
100. Suksi, M. (2022). Artificial intelligence and courts: Lessons from Estonia.
101. Supreme People's Court of China. (2020). *Smart court white paper.*
102. Supreme People's Court of China. (2023). *Annual report on the application of artificial intelligence in courts.*
103. Surden, H. (2020). Artificial intelligence and law: An overview. *Georgia State University Law Review, 36*(5).
104. Susskind, R. (2019). *Online courts and the future of justice.* Oxford University Press.
105. Thomas, E., Miller, J., & Chen, L. (2023). AI in threat assessment: Preventing mass violence through behavioral analysis. *Journal of Law and Technology, 15*(2).
106. Tivari, V., Dasari, V. S. R., & Wang, J. (2025). Digital forensics in the age of large language models. *arXiv.*

107. Turing, A. M. (1950). Computing machinery and intelligence. *Mind, 49.*

108. UNICRI & INTERPOL. (2021). *AI for law enforcement: Opportunities and challenges.*

109. Verdoliva, L. (2020). Media forensics and deepfakes: An overview. *IEEE Journal of Selected Topics in Signal Processing, 14*(5).

110. Voigt, P., & Von dem Bussche, A. (2021). *The EU General Data Protection Regulation (GDPR): A practical guide.* Springer.

111. Wachter, S., Mittelstadt, B., & Floridi, L. (2017). Transparent, explainable, and accountable AI for robotics. *Science Robotics, 2*(6).

112. Weizenbaum, J. (1966). ELIZA—a computer program for the study of natural language communication between man and machine. *Communications of the ACM, 9*(1), 36–45.

113. Wexler, R. (2021). Transparency in algorithmic criminal evidence analysis. *Yale Law Journal Forum, 130.*

114. Williams, J. (2024). Satellite imagery and big data in anti-trafficking operations. *British Journal of Criminology, 64*(2).

115. Zhang, W. (2021). AI and judicial decision-making in China. *Tsinghua China Law Review.*

116. Zhang, Y. (2024). Deepfake detection in smart court systems: Challenges and solutions. *China Law & Technology Review, 8*(2).

117. European Commission. (2021). *Proposal for a regulation laying down harmonised rules on artificial intelligence (Artificial Intelligence Act).* Brussels: Publications Office of the European Union.

118. *European Law Blog. (2024). Predictive policing in the AI Act: Meaningful ban or paper* tiger? European Law Blog.

119. Landmark judgment from the Netherlands on digital welfare states and human rights. (2024). Open Global Rights.

120. Moynihan, C. (2020, February 10). Dutch court blocks use of algorithmic risk scoring system for welfare fraud detection. *Just Security.*

121. Privacy International. (2020). Dutch court ruling on SyRI. *Privacy International Reports.*

Online Sources:

1. European Commission. (2021). *Proposal for a Regulation of the European Parliament and of the Council laying down harmonised rules on Artificial Intelligence (Artificial Intelligence Act).* EUR-Lex. https://eur-lex.europa.eu/legal-content/EN/TXT/?uri=CELEX:52021PC0206
2. South Wales Police. (2019). *Response to judgment in Bridges v South Wales Police.* https://www.south-wales.police.uk
3. Wisconsin Supreme Court. (2016). *State v. Loomis – Opinion.* https://wicourts.gov

www.ingramcontent.com/pod-product-compliance
Lightning Source LLC
LaVergne TN
LVHW022312200926
848481LV00004B/1302